PRAYING

WITH THE ONE

YOU LOVE

PRAYING

WITH THE ONE

YOU LOVE

First Baptist Church
53953 CR 17
Bristol, IN 46507

ART HUNT

FOREWORD BY H. NORMAN WRIGHT

PRAYING WITH THE ONE YOU LOVE
published by Multnomah Books
a part of the Questar publishing family

© 1996 by Art Hunt

International Standard Book Number: 0-88070-891-3

Cover photograph by Mike Houska
Cover design by Kevin Keller

Printed in the United States of America

Unless otherwise noted, Scripture quotations are the author's own translation.

Also quoted:
The Holy Bible, New International Version (NIV)
© 1973, 1984 by International Bible Society,
used by permission of Zondervan Publishing House.

Today's English Version (TEV)

For information:
QUESTAR PUBLISHERS, INC.
POST OFFICE BOX 1720
SISTERS, OREGON 97759

96 97 98 99 00 01 02 03 — 10 9 8 7 6 5 4 3 2 1

CONTENTS

FOREWORD

Every now and then a book is published which fills a void left absent for too many years. Such is this volume with a title that captures the theme and purpose of the author's intent. With the publishing of this book, couples can no longer say, "We don't have any resource to help us learn how to pray."

The contents of this resource should answer any of the questions that couples struggle with, and perhaps haven't yet considered at this point in their marital journey. As you, the reader, travel through these pages you will find the suggestions creative as well as practical.

Couples reading and learning to pray together will discover a heightened intensity of intimacy in other areas of their lives as well.

Praying together as a couple will strengthen and enrich any marriage but can also bring healing to troubled relationships. Learning to pray together is an indispensable necessity for every couple and this book makes it possible.

Whether you've been married one year of fifty, following these guidelines can make a difference. I would like to see this book required reading for all engaged couples. What a difference that would make in the enrichment of a marriage!

ACKNOWLEDGMENTS

God has blessed me with many friends along the way, each giving something unique to this book. Since all good gifts come from God himself, I look upon each person who helped with this project as a gift from him.

This book is dedicated to my wife, Naomi; but I want to express my thanks to her as well. I can't imagine a better partner or closer friend. She unselfishly released me to write, always affirmed me, always believed in me. Thanks, Naomi. You're the best.

I will always be thankful to Steve Barclift, who proposed the book to Questar and believed it was worthy of publication. Thanks, Steve.

Any writer is immensely aided by a good editor. How grateful I am for Becky Durost Fish. Becky, your enthusiasm, your skill, your prayers, your laughter, and your encouragement actually made the editing process enjoyable! Much credit goes to you for the form the book has taken.

Thanks to Dave Kopp and the rest of the Questar family. You all proved to be kind and encouraging. Thank you for believing in the book and doing everything you could to help make it a success.

Thanks also to the many couples in my home church, Lighthouse Christian Center, with whom I have talked about praying together — the Wilsons, the McDonnells, the Dills, and others. What great examples of married love I see in you all!

I want to express my thanks to the Fox Island couples: Phil and Lilly Ness, Alan and Sarah Myron, Dave and Carolyn Snow, and Stan and Diana Thompson. I so much appreciated the fun and profitable evening we spent together talking about prayer. Thanks as well to Nancy Knowlton for a stimulating, meaningful conversation.

The faculty of Trinity Evangelical Divinity School proved to be encouraging and insightful. Since this book began as a major component of my Doctor of Ministries studies, I greatly benefited from the faculty's input.

I'm grateful to Tom White, author of *The Believer's Guide to Spiritual Warfare*. Tom graciously read and commented on chapter 9, "Resisting the Evil One." Thanks for your insight, Tom.

My friend Gail Aardappel gave an early draft of this book a crucial proofreading. Thanks, Gail — you saved me a lot of time.

Finally, I am grateful to my Lord. He put the vision for this book in my heart, and provided the resources to make it happen. As good comes from it, the credit belongs to him. Thank you, Father, for all you have provided, including the good gifts of the many who helped me.

Whether you've been married for fifty years or still planning your honeymoon, you've probably experienced a desire for spiritual intimacy — a deep longing for your partner in marriage to become your partner in prayer. For almost ten years I've encouraged couples to develop a prayer life together. I'm convinced that part of the great Christian movements sweeping across our land — from Prayer Summits to Promise Keepers — is aimed squarely at couples. God wants marriage partners to join together in prayer and experience the joy, the satisfaction, and the dynamic power that comes from such unions. He is moving to create potent spiritual partnerships within marriages all over this country. That's what this book is all about. Intrigued? Then please read on!

How to Use This Book

The purpose of this book is to help couples develop or expand a prayer life together. It will stimulate discussion and encourage couples not only to think about spiritual union, but also to cultivate their prayer life together. In the weeks to come, God can do something wonderful in your marriage as you commit yourself to growing in this area.

Each chapter offers practical help and advice that will draw couples together in their new prayer venture. I suggest that you read the material out loud together, or that both partners read a chapter independently and then discuss the concept presented. An exercise is provided at the end of each chapter to help you communicate your thoughts to each other and then become more open to the idea of praying together. Some couples may think the exercises seem artificial or make them feel uncomfortable. That's okay. If the questions help you start discussions, great! If you find you have no difficulty talking about the material presented, the exercises may be unnecessary. Do what is most natural and helpful for you as a couple. But by all means, begin and continue that discussion in any way that works for you.

In my prayer seminars for couples, I usually ask participants, "What are your expectations for our time together?" I hear comments like, "We want a place to begin a new commitment to pray together," or "We want to gain some new tools so that we can create common ground in this area," or "We want to get over the current speed bump that seems to be such an obstacle in our prayer life."

Perhaps you have similar expectations. I believe that if you ask God to use this book in your life, you too can find spiritual renewal in your marriage, and a rewarding prayer life together. Is that what you desire? With God's help, it can become a reality.

CHAPTER ONE

What Happens When Couples Pray?

Though one may be overpowered, two can defend themselves.
A cord of three strands is not quickly broken.

ECCLESIASTES 4:12

SOMETHING DYNAMIC HAPPENS to our marriages when we decide to pray. When we commit with our partners to come before God, we open the door to new and exciting changes that will bless us like nothing before.

Perhaps you're ready to join hands and hearts to explore a new level of fellowship and worship within your marriage. Do you long to experience God in a bigger way? Or maybe you resonate with the words of John of the Cross, a sixteenth-century friar, whose simple prayer eloquently expresses his desire for God:

> I no longer want just to hear about you, beloved Lord, through messengers. I no longer want to hear doctrines about you, nor to have my emotions stirred by people speaking of you. I yearn for your presence. The love which you show in glimpses, reveal to me fully.[1]

As you discover more of God, he'll lead you to discover more about yourself and your spouse. Take the example of Tom and Catherine. More than anything, they wanted to deepen their spiritual lives together. They decided to go on a weekend retreat, and then continued to seek God together the following week. At first they felt awkward about praying together, but gradually they found themselves opening up. Listen to an excerpt from Catherine's journal describing this experience:

> Monday morning began with our individual daily quiet times, followed by our time of united prayer. We'd asked God to remove any barriers to our communion with him, and with one another. And this he began to do on Monday afternoon. He opened a badly festered yet hidden wound and gently drained the poison amidst our buckets of tears.[2]

This was only the beginning, but Tom and Catherine continued in their quest and found what they were looking for: a deepening relationship with God and each other. They developed a stronger sense of trust and commitment as they poured out their hearts to God. Simply put, they sought God together in prayer, and as a result they became closer to their Father and closer to each other.

Tom and Catherine experienced what countless other couples have learned: When Christian couples pray together, they experience extraordinary benefits. Antoine de Saint-Exupéry observed that "to love does not mean simply to look at one another, but to look together in the same direction."[3] We love our spouses in the most basic way when we both look together toward God.

As we kneel side by side before God, we invite him to invade our marriages with power and love and healing. King Solomon's words in Ecclesiastes 4:12 suggest an appropriate symbol for prayer in marriage: "Though one may be overpowered, two can defend themselves. A cord of three strands is not quickly broken." In the ancient world, a rope was formed and strengthened as individual strands were twisted together. In the same way, couples who invite the Lord into their relationship through prayer find their lives uniquely interwoven. Each strand — husband, wife, and God himself — combines with the others to form a strong cord that will withstand the many forces that can unravel a marriage relationship.

Simplistic answers are sometimes offered as formulas for successful marriages. Do this or do that and satisfaction is guaranteed. But common sense tells us that each couple is different and no one method will work for every marriage. I won't add to the glut of pat answers for tough questions. But at the same time, my experience with couples of all ages makes one simple principle about marriage very clear: *Praying together as a couple can improve and strengthen every marriage, and at the same time deepen the couple's relationship to God.* "A chord of three strands is not quickly broken."

In twenty years of marriage to my wife, Naomi, praying together has enriched our relationship beyond anything I could have imagined back when we said our vows at the alter. This is the same testimony shared by hundreds of other couples that I've met over the years.

Dick and Colette are typical. They've only been married for two years, but they committed to pray together right in their car on the way to their honeymoon. Dick said, "We wanted to involve God immediately in our marriage." In the two years since, praying together has become the cornerstone of their relationship. Dick sums up their experience this way: "Jesus Christ is our best friend."

When you pray together, you give God priority in your

relationship. This emphasis is like an open door — an invitation for God to enter and deepen his presence in your marriage.

What a Difference It Makes

Over the years, I've invited Christian couples to describe what's so powerful about praying together. They come from various backgrounds and have different personalities, temperaments, and ages; yet these couples all share an extraordinary closeness and joy in their marriage. And all attribute this amazing difference to their ongoing spiritual journey together.

One couple, married for forty-three years, told me they'd prayed together from the time they became Christians. The wife remarked: "There was a period of two or three years when we didn't pray together, and our marriage wasn't nearly as vital or sweet. We decided to go back to prayer, and we've been at it ever since." This couple had seen a lot in forty-three years — both good and bad — and they knew that prayer was a must.

Another wife told me recently, "There's a security in our relationship when we pray together. I have much more peace when we agree together for our lives." Perhaps this is because praying together reminds us of our commitment to God. That commitment reaffirms our marriage vow and touches a deep cord. When you pray together, not only are your personal spiritual needs met, but your marriage relationship is enfolded in God's arms as well.

One husband told me simply, "The bottom line is this: Praying together improves our relationship." That, of course, is what all Christian couples want: a relationship that's healthy and growing. This husband discovered that when he prays with his spouse their relationship deepens and strengthens in a remarkable way.

Even this morning, as Naomi and I enjoyed our prayer time, I became aware again of the difference prayer makes in our marriage. We started out, as usual, by expressing thanks to God, then turned our attention from ourselves to our Lord. After a while, Naomi confessed her need for God to keep her spiritually focused. I hadn't even known she felt that way. As she prayed, I gained insight into her life and was able to pray with her about her concerns. It was a pleasant reminder of how important this time was for connecting our lives spiritually — without that moment I might not have known how she felt about an important aspect of her life. Because of that time together, I gained a keen sense of alignment with her and a confidence that God is at work. As we agreed in prayer, I knew we were in unity and God was already involved.

After we finished praying together, we both felt a tremendous sense of well-being — our burdens were left in God's hands. We spontaneously hugged, and felt God's arms around us. We couldn't help but notice how we were both filled with an even deeper love for God, and for each other. It's still amazing how, after all these years, it keeps getting better and better.

Like a painting in progress, the benefits of praying together build with each spiritual brush stroke. Something beautiful is created. When our daily prayer times end, we always look forward to something good and fulfilling.

What happens when couples pray? Many things, all of them good. Marriages are enriched — some are literally transformed! Couples who share a prayer life together discover that the time, commitment, energy, and risk are all very worthwhile. Prayer definitely makes a difference!

The Designer's Plan

God designed us to pray together. He makes this plan known in a general sense through the Bible's instruction to pray for one another. In James 5:16 it's clear: "Therefore confess your sins to each other and pray for each other so that you may be healed." When the New Testament speaks of intercession, it encourages believers to first pray for each other. Acts 12:5 is another example of the early church "earnestly praying to God" for another believer.

As Christian couples, we experience God's design for the body of Christ in our marriage. Sometimes we forget that our husbands or wives are, first of all, our brothers or sisters in Christ, and that we can operate as the body of Christ in our homes. God has already given us a wonderful tool to help us develop a strong spiritual partnership: prayer.

First Peter 3:7 shows us the important status of prayer in God's blueprint for our lives:

> *Husbands, in the same way be considerate as you live with your wives, and treat them with respect as the weaker partner and as heirs with you of the gracious gift of life, so that nothing will hinder your prayers.*

The Greek word for "your" in this verse is plural. Dr. Grant Osborne, professor of New Testament at Trinity Evangelical Divinity School, suggests the phrase "nothing will hinder your prayer" might be translated, "so that nothing will interfere with your prayers or your prayers as a couple."[4]

Listen to what writer and theologian Alan M. Stibbs wrote about this passage:

> He should, therefore, live with her as a man fully aware that, in addition to the natural enjoyment of each other, they are,

as Christians, *called together to a spiritual fellowship with God* and Christ, a sphere in which his wife is not weaker or inferior, but a joint-heir. Only if this delicately balanced fellowship between husband and wife is thus properly maintained will their union reach its true Christian fulfillment. *For such a partnership is meant to be especially fruitful, not only physically in having children, but also spiritually in praying together and in seeing prayer answered* [italics added].[5]

Another familiar scriptural principle supports prayer in marriage: the one flesh joining of a man and woman through the marriage covenant. This one-flesh union is first mentioned in Genesis 2:24 and is developed throughout the New Testament. Numerous Bible teachers have observed that the original Hebrew phrase for "one flesh" goes beyond mere physical union to mean a *total* union: body, soul, and spirit. Jesus adds in the Gospels that such a one-flesh covenant is an indication that God himself has joined a man and woman together in a permanent spiritual bond (Matthew 19:6).

If we wish to enjoy such a close union we must relate to and be in relationship with God *as a couple.* When we become one, that "one" now has a special status before God. If we take seriously the "one flesh" covenant, praying together will be a natural result.

So What's the Big Deal?

Is there really a need to talk about this? Don't most Christian couples already pray together? What's so hard about it, anyway?

Some years ago I distributed a questionnaire to one hundred adult Christians who were part of a large Sunday school class in a suburban church. All of the people were married — although some spouses chose not to participate. I hoped to gain some insight into the need for couples to pray together.

I was fascinated by the results. Almost everyone indicated an intellectual commitment to the importance of prayer. They all agreed with the need to pray with their spouse. They understood the potential benefit to their spiritual lives and marriage. Yet twenty-two percent of those who responded said that they *never* prayed with their spouse. Another thirty-two percent said that they occasionally prayed with their spouse for less than five minutes. *Altogether, over fifty percent of the respondents had virtually no prayer life whatsoever with their spouse.*

It's these couples that concern me the most: those who have never fully experienced the positive impact of prayer on their marriage; those whose life's crises are handled without the comfort of united prayer; those who are consumed by screaming urgencies and yet neglect one of God's greatest helps.

Is there a need? Absolutely. Since that first questionnaire, my informal research continues to reveal the same dismal conclusions. There are as many reasons for this as there are couples. Even those who don't pray together recognize their need to do so. And many still long to forge a spiritual life together, but don't know how.

While many Christian marriages aren't in immediate danger, they may need revitalization. These couples miss out on some of the joy of partnership, and their spiritual journey is a lonely one. Perhaps worst of all, they never experience the deepest level of spiritual intimacy that God has planned for them. But if they learn to pray with their loved one and address some of the issues that have inhibited them in the past, they will experience many benefits.

Take a moment to think about your marriage. Do you ever take the time to join together in prayer? If you don't pray as a couple, what keeps you from it? Is it safe enough to pray? Is it fear of intimacy? Lack of time? Lack of motivation? The rest of this chapter deals with one of the most often mentioned obstacles to prayer in marriage: no one takes responsibility to see that it happens.

We're All in This Together

For a number of years, Martha told Dave she wanted to pray with him. Often her requests resulted in a brief time of prayer together. But always, the initiative was hers. Finally, Martha became so irritated by Dave's apparent lack of interest that she stopped asking. Prayer left their marriage.

Dave told me he actually wanted to pray with Martha, but it was always easier to let her take full responsibility. When she stopped asking about prayer, he simply let the issue slide.

Martha and Dave aren't alone. Many couples say the reason they don't pray together is because no one leads the way.

It helps when we accept and understand that *praying together is a joint responsibility.* Since we all benefit from prayer in our marriages, we need to share the load — we need to help each other make prayer a part of our daily lives. Peter described believers as a "holy priesthood" (1 Peter 2:5). This concept is developed further in Revelation 1:6 where Jesus calls believers "a kingdom and priests to serve his God and Father."

Even within our one-flesh partnership, there's call for each partner to move in the direction God has shown them. As husbands and wives, we need to come to a place of agreement — a place where prayer is a priority.

Holding Back

In the last two decades, our understanding of mutual submission in marriage has been under the spotlight. As a result, many men have overcorrected and, consequently, neglect their God-given responsibility to lead in the family. Men too often allow their wives to take full responsibility for the spiritual atmosphere of the home.

Perhaps you are tired of hearing about God and yearn for his presence.

Like a painting in progress, the benefits of praying together build with each spiritual brush stroke.

When you pray together your marriage is enriched — some marriages are transformed.

In Ephesians 5 the husband is called the "head of the wife." Whatever their understanding of headship, most men desire to nurture the spiritual side of their marriage. Many times, however, praying together just doesn't happen. I understand this. Life whirls by at an incredible pace. You have many responsibilities, and each one is important. You need, though, to consider what is holding you back. As you read this book, think clearly about your situation and talk to your wife about what keeps you from taking the lead.

Many men express having difficulties in this area. One husband stated it this way: "I knew if I failed at leading my wife into prayer, I had failed at the biblical model for husbands. And I felt guilty about it. It sure wasn't easy at the beginning. It's a continual learning process. It feels comfortable now, but it wasn't to start with."

Perseverance pays off! It did for this husband. What was uncomfortable to start with became comfortable because he stayed with it. Most of us husbands want to lead our wives into prayer, but certain things may hold us back. Perhaps you're afraid to open up, or maybe you just don't know how. We'll discuss ways to deal with these and other obstacles in the chapters to come. Why not tackle these issues and put them behind you, so you can begin praying with the one you love?

Feeling Alone

When husbands don't share in the responsibility to make prayer a part of their marriage, wives can feel very alone. They may become discouraged and quit trying. Sadly sometimes they stop caring. If this is your situation, here are some techniques that may help.

Communicate directly with your husband. One woman frequently compares her marriage to another couple's in the church. "Look how they pray together," she says to her husband. It's an indirect way of saying, "Get with it."

A better approach is to communicate directly, without blame, using "I" messages: Direct words that communicate what *you* feel or think rather than guessing about your spouse's motivation. The idea is to describe your spouse's *behavior* and what emotions are aroused by that behavior.

"I" messages look like this: "When you [describe behavior of spouse], I feel [describe the emotion that goes on inside you]." You might say, "Jim, when weeks go by and we haven't prayed together, I begin to feel anxious and out of touch with you. It would mean so much to me if you would make prayer with me a priority." Keep in mind that finding the right time and place can be as important as saying it right. When you are sure you've chosen the right moment, communicate your thoughts as directly as you can.

If you feel discouraged about this area of your marriage, consider these words of a husband who has been married for many years: "I can remember that we started to pray together because she said we needed to. She reminded me, 'We really ought to pray.' Without the reminder, who knows how much longer it would have taken?"

When I asked him if her reminders made him angry, he said: "No, but I did feel guilty. My wife was never unkind to me. When she talked to me, I felt, 'That's my responsibility; I need to take care of it.' "

Why didn't this husband react negatively? I think the answer has something to do with the wife's motivation. If we bring up issues for the purpose of changing our spouse, we will cause more harm than good.

Psychologist Larry Crabb has much to say about motivation in his book *The Marriage Builder.* We can monitor our motivation by recognizing what we feel if our spouse does *not* cooperate. If we feel a lingering sense of anger or depression or anxiety, our goal may have been to change our mate. If instead we are looking out for our spouse's well-being, we primarily will feel sorrow if they don't cooperate.

Communicate with God. Even if your partner is not taking the lead, you need to stay in contact with the Lord. First, this is a way of continuing to grow as an individual and maintaining your own spiritual life. When a husband blocks spiritual intimacy, a wife loses something precious. Naturally there are feelings associated with such a loss. God cares about these emotions. He wants to hear about them. Be yourself as you come before God. Don't stop with the expression of your feelings, though. Ask God to give you perspective. Ask him to help you move in his direction. If you listen, God will both comfort you and bring you strength.

Second, in prayer you need to forgive your spouse. Almost without your realizing it, a gnawing anger can begin to work its way into your life. Bitterness can be the result. Forgiveness is simply deciding in prayer to release your husband from the debt he owes you. You may need to do this on an ongoing basis, but it must be done.

Finally, your communication with God includes praying *for* your husband. In 2 Thessalonians 1:11, God promises that he will "fulfill every good purpose of yours and every act prompted by your faith." Praying for your husband is a good purpose! Be specific in your requests for your husband, but also be guided by the Holy Spirit.

Are We Too Far Gone?

You may be thinking that in your marriage, prayer just won't work. Perhaps it's a case of believing "If we can't *talk* together, we certainly can't *pray* together."

Such sentiments contain some truth. If you have problems in your marriage, praying as a couple is not a cure-all. It's not meant to be a release from or cover-up of your responsibilities as a wife or husband. But prayer is healthy and helpful for a Christian couple, no matter where they are in their relationship. Certainly, praying together changes as a couple becomes more intimate. But it can be an asset at any time in a marriage, even when a couple is experiencing relationship difficulties.

Some time ago, Carol and Larry Zetterberg described in *Guideposts* how praying together became a pathway of healing for their marriage. The Zetterbergs' marriage was in deep trouble when God dropped this thought into Carol's mind: *Pray for Larry.* She resisted, but as their marriage got worse she began to pray for her husband. And finally, she asked Larry to pray with her. To her amazement, he agreed.

They had no idea how to pray at first, and were hesitant and awkward. Carol suggested that to start with, each of them could write down on a piece of paper what they wanted the other to pray about. That's what they did. They then exchanged lists, sat down together in a big, overstuffed chair, and prayed. This is what Carol had to say about the episode:

> Clumsily, we got through it — each praying for the other's requests. I was amazed at how touched I was to hear Larry praying for me. I couldn't remember the last time I'd heard someone pray just for my concerns.[6]

This couple discovered tremendous benefits from prayer. It became the instrument that healed their marriage. Will this be every couple's experience? No. However, for those couples who say, "We fight all the time; how can we pray?" this can be an encouragement. Our Father can intervene at any point in a marriage, helping couples draw near to God and to each other through shared prayer.

All this may sound so nebulous, so difficult to you. Perhaps you feel confused and intimidated before you even begin. But obstacles to prayer can be overcome! This book can be an important step toward developing the prayer life together that you've always wanted. I hope you'll enter in with great enthusiasm and hopeful expectations — this could be the start of an amazing spiritual honeymoon as you begin to pray with the one you love!

The next section includes some exercises to lead you closer to your goal. Each chapter will contain the same format and I encourage you to use it in the way that works best for you. Each couple is unique — some enjoy taking on new activities one step at a time, while others prefer to leap into things and figure it out later. My hope is that these questions will get the conversation started and draw you closer together. For this first exercise, I'd like to share some basic guidelines. Good communication needs nurturing and the following three steps will start you off right:

• *Physical closeness.* Bypass your favorite recliner or rocker and opt to sit together, *knee-to-knee* on the couch, at the kitchen table, or on your bed. Knee-to-knee means you face each other. Without the benefit of eye-to-eye contact, a wealth of non-verbal communication, or body language, is missed.

• *Real listening.* This means you focus on what your spouse is saying without forming your response simultaneously. It's okay to take time to respond — agree that a pause is only a pause — not a hidden message. It helps to paraphrase or repeat back what you think your spouse has said.

• *Open mind and heart.* The purpose of sharing isn't to determine rightness or to win another to your way of thinking. It's simply to better understand each other. And to accept each other.

(Keep in mind, written questions sometimes put your brain on the spot—have you ever drawn a complete blank? For this reason "prompters" are included with some questions. These are meant to trigger your thinking, not replace it.)

How'd We Get Here?

You've begun to read a book about talking to God together. By doing so, you've turned the knob and cracked open the door to your prayer "closet". Are you ready to invite your partner into this intimate space? What brought you to the place where you can even open this door? Why do you desire to pray together? These are important questions for each partner to answer right up front.

Otherwise, misunderstanding or cross purposes might cause you to slam your "closet" door shut before it's completely open. Take a moment to share why you've come to this place — why you want to pray together.

Where We're At *(both answer)*

1. For the partner who picked out this book: Honestly tell your spouse why it caught your attention and caused you to spend money on it (or borrow it). Explain why you've invited your spouse to read it with you.

2. For the partner who's been asked to go through this book: Honestly tell your spouse your initial reaction to the request. What thoughts led you to agree to do this?

A Step Forward *(both answer)*

1. Is it hard for you to take responsibility for prayer — or the lack of it?

2. If so, why?

Prompter: Am I convinced that God really wants us to pray together...

3. Brainstorm ideas for dealing with responsibility issues.

Prompter: Write ideas down. Are responsibilities shared in a way that both partners feel is comfortable? Do you need to let go of some things?

"Closet" Action

In the presence of your spouse, be honest with God about your attitude toward praying together and the thing(s) that make taking responsibility for it hard. Ask God for help where needed.

CHAPTER TWO

Getting Closer to the One You Love

For this reason a man will leave his father and mother and be united to his wife, and they will become one flesh.
GENESIS 2:24

I ENJOY PERFORMING WEDDING CEREMONIES. Over the years I've been involved in many. Yet I always experience a sense of awe each time two people are joined together to become one. Their ceremony is a declaration that a lasting bond has been created. And we, the observers, are allowed to witness that holy event. Usually I go home to my wife with eyes still soft, heart still glowing at the wonder of what has transpired!

Then I remember this couple will go immediately to a honeymoon. And suddenly my emotions shift as I consider how those two newlyweds now face a permanent commitment — the closest bond possible between two human beings. It's almost overwhelming! How will they handle such intimacy? Mike Mason captures the dilemma well:

Everywhere else, throughout society there are fences, walls, burglar alarms, unlisted numbers, the most elaborate precautions for helping people keep at a safe distance. But in marriage all of that is reversed. In marriage the walls are down, and not only do the man and woman live under the same roof, but they sleep under the same covers.[1]

Many people fear such intimacy. The prospect of all their protective walls coming down seems too much to handle. Certainly, praying together is an equally intimate behavior. Try to visualize a couple sitting in bed together praying. Can you see them? If you can't imagine them, perhaps you can hear them. Is it a comfortable image? Or does it make you want to close your eyes and shut your ears? What feelings surface in you — anxiety? peace? apathy? Think about it. How easy would it be for you to be transparent and genuine in a time of prayer with your partner?

Getting a Little Closer

One time, early in our marriage, Naomi and I prayed together, and she shared her anguish with the Lord about a situation that burdened her. Suddenly I realized how much she must trust me. As she prayed, I could tell she was being very real and candidly honest with the Lord — she spoke of feelings, needs, and hurts, and she did so in front of me. When it was my turn to pray, I felt encouraged to be more vulnerable too.

What is it that builds intimacy in a marriage? How do we go about learning to trust the other with our most private thoughts and emotions when we've been independent so long? To start with, one spouse must take the risky step of disclosing something very personal — maybe even painful. In other words, they lay their heart on the line. And when their partner responds with open understanding and acceptance, a new layer of trust and intimacy is built into their relationship.

When I express something to my wife that is deeply significant to me, I take a small risk of rejection. I am revealing a part of myself — a part she may or may not understand. Yet when she listens to me with empathy and expresses acceptance, I feel affirmed. Not that she must always agree with me — acceptance is not the same as agreement. But when I am allowed to be me, I begin to feel safe, and my trust in Naomi deepens. That trust allows me to go even deeper next time, and as this process repeats, it builds our level of intimacy.

Praying with your spouse is perhaps the most intimate thing you can do together. Think of what happens when you pray. There you are, right in front of God — and he can see right through you! And there by your side, is your partner. You are both literally "unveiled" before God. You may have already said "I trust you" to your spouse, but this — mutual prayer — is where the real risk comes into play. Is it worth it? Ask risk-takers why they take risks and they will tell you it's because of the possible gains. The bigger the risk, the bigger the reward. And in this case the reward is enormous!

One husband confessed to me that he was a loner when he first married his wife. "Prayer to me was a private thing," he said. "But the thing that has made the greatest difference in our lives as a couple is my willingness to be vulnerable with her through prayer." Because this husband was willing to be vulnerable, a prayer life developed that made a great difference in their almost thirty years of marriage.

When a couple prays together, they cannot help but grow more intimate in their relationship. When we risk with our partner and are accepted, we're willing to risk again. And each time we risk and are accepted, the intimacy level in our marriage increases. Before long a couple will operate on a level where they are willing to trust each other with many more areas of their inner lives. I never feel warmer, safer, or closer to Naomi than after times of prayer — when we have touched God, been real in his presence, and prayed for and with each other.

Intimacy also grows because as we pray together, we come to know each other better. One husband, married for nine years, told me, "My wife was praying one night and expressed a deep feeling to God. I thought, *Really?* I learned something I never would've known." Another husband said simply, "Prayer helps our communication. I hear things in prayer that I don't even know about my wife. And sometimes our prayer sparks an important conversation."

Genesis 2:18–25 is the first text on marriage in the Bible. The kind of marriage bond described in this passage is very intimate. Genesis 2:25 says, "The man and his wife were both naked and were not ashamed." There was perfect ease between them: no fear of rejection, no pretense, no defense, no walls. Can you imagine a relationship with no fear or inhibition? It's that kind of intimacy that God desires for all married couples.

Don't Get Too Close to Me

Fear of intimacy is an obvious barrier to closeness. So naturally, this fear can be a formidable hurdle to praying with a mate. My experience with couples indicates again and again that spiritual intimacy can be scary! Some couples just can't seem to let the walls come down.

Often there are legitimate reasons for walls. Maybe one time we took the risk of revealing who we are and were hurt. Perhaps we don't feel accepted in some area of life, or have felt the sting of rejection.

History and old wounds can be hard to overcome. But regardless of where our fear comes from, it will always be an obstacle to getting closer. Fear is the great inhibitor in marriage. Yet if we believe that God's "perfect love drives out fear"(1 John 4:18), perhaps we can also learn how our mate's love can do the same.

Why James Bond Doesn't Bond

Men more often fear intimacy than women do. In fact, this section could be titled "Why Men Are Afraid to Pray with Their Wives." There are many reasons men sometimes have a hard time learning to pray with their wives. To start with, many men were encouraged to hide their feelings for most of their lives. When an eight-year-old boy falls and cuts his knee, he typically hears, "Be a big boy, now. Don't cry." Or on a camping trip, when a small boy is afraid to cross a small stream on stepping stones, he will hear: "Come on, don't be afraid. Big boys are brave!" Many of us guys grew up with that macho-male image that was personified by the Marlborough Man, James Bond, and Clint Eastwood. The message they conveyed was: Don't say how you really feel. Now here we are in the nineties, and we're supposed to express ourselves and become *open*. No matter how much we want to, it's not always easy to undo a lifetime of "tough-guy" habits. And then of course there are even physical differences in the brain that may contribute to men being less in touch with their feelings than women.

Consider the average twelve-year-old girl, spending the night at a friend's house. What does she talk about all night? Her feelings; the boy she's in love with; her dreams for the future; her hurts and disappointments. Now think of two twelve-year-old boys spending the night together. They talk about *things*. They report facts — relating to sports, school and what they want to do tomorrow — then they go to sleep.

Many times we men are afraid of what we are feeling. How can we tell others what we ourselves are desperately hiding away? In *The Secrets Men Keep,* Ken Druck makes the point that we "block off entire areas of ourselves, stamp them 'TOP SECRET,' and file them away. And we keep their very existence a secret from wives, girlfriends, children and buddies. We see these parts of who we are as a threat. Perhaps they embarrass us. Or maybe they fail to confirm a particular image we have set out to project for others."[2]

Druck goes on to discuss the nature of the secrets men keep locked up inside; in these areas they fail to open themselves to honest disclosure. But there is power in disclosure. Men can choose to open themselves up to their wives.

A Little Understanding Goes a Long Way

If your partner fears intimacy, if he or she finds it difficult to draw close to you, you need to demonstrate special understanding. Try to discover the level of transparency that your spouse can handle. Your partner doesn't have to take a giant leap toward intimacy in order to pray with you. Offer lots of support as your spouse takes small steps toward the ideal. By the same token, be gracious if he or she is uncomfortable with the level of intimacy you want. Most of all, give it time.

Listen to one husband's story:

I've always been a loner. The issue of praying with my wife was not something that ever came to me. I started by simply reading the Bible to her at night. Once you read the Bible, what do you do? You must at least say 'Amen.' Prayer started through that avenue and didn't become consistent until some time later.

This man's wife was wise enough to allow her husband some room. Because she did, he was able eventually to move toward her and overcome his fears. Prayer became a tool in opening the door to emotional intimacy for this couple.

For those who struggle with low self-esteem, emotional or spiritual intimacy may feel like nakedness to them. They may feel the need to cover themselves and hide. For some, the intimacy of intercourse is easier to achieve than revealing something private about themselves. This isn't God's ideal. Remember the words at the close of Adam and Eve's "marriage ceremony"? "They were naked and unashamed." There were no barriers. We sometimes feel that if our mates were to see us as we really are, we would be ashamed. Yet the most powerful moment in an intimate relationship is when our shame is met with acceptance and love. When we reveal who we really are and yet are affirmed, healing takes place, and we discover that the risk was worthwhile.

Echoes from the Past

We sometimes fear intimacy because of how we were raised. If our parents didn't provide sufficient affirmation and a safe place to grow up, we may need to work harder on issues of trust and getting close to others. Psychiatrist M. Scott Peck has observed:

> Whenever there is a major deficit in parental love, the child will, in all likelihood, respond to that deficit by assuming itself to be the cause of the deficit, thereby developing an unrealistically negative self-image.[3]

We commonly accept as true the hypothesis that we must love ourselves in order to love others. But sometimes we forget how a negative self-image can ruin a relationship. When we're unsure of ourselves we find it very difficult to reveal our true self to others. We want to hide. This lack of self-esteem always inhibits our openness to intimacy. We become captive to thoughts like: "It's not safe to show people who I really am. I would be laughed at. I might even be rejected." For some, to reveal their inner-most feelings would be to give another person power over them. And that is intolerable to them.

Gary Smalley and John Trent talk about homes that withhold a blessing from their children; homes where a critical parent or demanding attitude prevent the child from gaining nurturing words, an accepting touch, or unconditional caring.[4] Children of such homes grow up fearing closeness while, at the same time, desperately wanting it. When they marry, they often expect their spouse to supply everything their parents didn't.

We need to realize how past experiences affect our marriages. We may have learned to fear because we grew up in an environment where it wasn't safe to be ourselves. The way we see ourselves as adults has been impacted by the way our parents and other important people accepted or rejected us. A history of rejection teaches us to "keep to ourselves" and "play it safe" rather than risk rejection.

Take Jack, for example. He was the black sheep of his family. His father was a successful professional, and his brothers followed suit; but Jack had held a number of jobs over the last fifteen years. All of Jack's life he had heard one message from his father: You are a disappointment.

When Jack married, he hoped he had at last found someone to

affirm him, yet he prepared himself from the beginning to be rejected. At the first sign of disapproval or questioning, Jack pulled back from his wife. He assumed his wife was just like his dad.

Jack needed to learn that while his father had failed to affirm him, other people wouldn't necessarily do the same. As Jack dealt with his negative history, he began to realize that he often set himself up for rejection by assuming the worst in new relationships. Soon he recognized that he was actually rejecting others before they rejected him.

Perhaps you can picture or feel old hurts which prevent you from reaching out to your spouse. It's never too late to change the way you think. But you must choose to make some new and healthy assumptions, like: "I *am* capable of having a successful and mutually satisfying relationship with my spouse. My partner is *not* waiting to reject me. God *will* help me build intimacy with my spouse as I take risks."

We long for a safe place, a relationship where we can be real and still be accepted.

When we share this prayer relationship as a couple, intimacy is measured not with a teaspoon — but with a shovel!

Whether prayer is breathed out during the high energy foot race of life or poured out in the quiet of early morning devotions, communion with God is at its heart.

If you can, talk directly to your spouse about your childhood. Without casting blame, try to focus on things your spouse may say or do that trigger old feelings and make you want to shut down. Explain those feelings, and how they have developed over time. Then make a commitment to reveal more and more of who you are to your partner. Most of all, allow the one you love to make mistakes without assuming it means rejection.

Overcoming Poor Self-Image

Self-esteem, self-worth, self-image — we hear these terms all the time. But how do we change the way we see ourselves? How do we break a lifetime of bad habits — like comparing ourselves to others, putting ourselves down, or giving up too easily?

Many books have been generated on this topic over the last few years, some of them excellently done.[5] Briefly, there are four ways to improve self-esteem in the context of marriage: 1) commit to telling yourself the truth about yourself as revealed by God's Word; 2) act upon that truth; 3) share your fear with your spouse; and 4) ask God for his help.

First, tell yourself the truth about yourself. Too often we base our self-worth on our performance and the opinions of others. Believe me, that's a prescription for pain! All of us fail, after all, and people's opinions are notoriously fickle. You may have lived all your life under the cloud of others' inaccurate assessments. Perhaps you've spent much of your time desperately trying to please someone, to gain their affirmation so that you can somehow be counted worthy.

Such "guiding fiction" can have disastrous effects on our lives. A guiding fiction is the lie we tell ourselves about how to be significant, how to gain worth. It usually goes something like this: "If I just perform well enough, my (husband, wife, mother, friend) will affirm me and approve of me, and *then* I will be worthwhile." A guiding fiction is just that — a lie.

Years ago, I ministered to a woman, fifty-eight years old, who had lived all her life trying to please her mother. She believed that if she could only perform well enough, her mother would finally give what she had never given — her approval. She would literally do anything her mother asked, hoping for a few crumbs of affirmation. After several months of counseling, this woman began to feel free of her guiding fiction. And for the first time in her life she experienced God's unconditional love. She was then able to make important changes in her relationships based on the truth she had learned about herself.

The most reliable facts about God's children come from his Word. *God's* opinion is what matters most. We need to clearly understand what his Word says about us. Romans 8:31–39 indicates that we are unconditionally loved. What can separate us from God's love? Nothing. God's love is ours, and there's nothing we can do about it. God will never reject us for any reason.

Romans 5:8 is one of my favorite passages about God's love: "But God demonstrates his own love for us in this: While we were still sinners, Christ died for us." God's love touched us before we had anything to give in return. God's love is never built around our performance; it is given without condition. *That* is God's grace — his loving kindness — and it is freely extended to every believer. Parents, friends, even spouses may base their love for us on how well we perform. But God's grace will never allow him to do anything but love us. We need to tell ourselves the truth — that we are unconditionally loved by our Father in heaven.

The Bible also indicates that "we are God's workmanship, created in Christ Jesus to do good works" (Ephesians 2:10). Each of us is the work of God's hands, created by him. That gives every individual intrinsic value. Imagine the great paintings of the world. Each has a signature: Rembrandt, Monet, Picasso. The paintings have value in part due to the signature they bear. In the same way, every individual has God's "signature." We are God's workmanship — an original. As Psalms 139 says, we are "fearfully and wonderfully made" by God himself.

Not only are we God's workmanship, but he gave each of us purpose in life: We were created for "good works." God is an "equal opportunity employer"; the work he has for us to do is not based on education, experience, gender, or any other condition. We qualify just as we are. We are important to God! He made us; he has gifted us; he wants to use our lives to impact others.

Of course, most of us know we are loved and important. After all, the Bible is quite clear on that. While most of us *know* these facts, many of us don't *tell ourselves* these truths. It's like listening to an old, distorted tape over and over when we have access to new tapes. Those new recordings won't do us any good unless we *play* them. In the same way, many Christians know the truth about themselves but when situations arrive which threaten their worth, they play the old tape in their mind, full of self-deprecating, performance-oriented messages.

My point? Make a commitment to tell yourself the truth. Say, for example, that you're praying with your spouse. You're somewhat awkward and make a few verbal mistakes. The old tape would play: "Oh no, that sounds so stupid! She/he probably thinks I'm foolish." Instead, play *this* tape: "I know who I am in Christ — I'm loved and important in him. I feel disappointed when I make mistakes, but I can choose to stay vulnerable because I know who I am!"

Tell yourself the truth. Write out Bible verses that talk about God's love for you and memorize them. Develop a new "recording," based on those Scriptures, and repeat it often enough to make it your own. Mentally challenge thoughts which run counter to God's Word. Ask God to help you tell yourself the truth.

This requires effort. It's not easy to crawl out from under the lies that want to imprison us. Some of us may need the help of a professional counselor to successfully change our thought patterns. That's okay. Regardless of what it takes to get the job done, we must begin to see ourselves as God does.

Second, choose to act upon the new way of thinking. If we are loved and important, then it's possible to take risks. After all, the risk may result in a closer relationship with your spouse. In situations wherein you are not affirmed or accepted, remember who you are in Christ. Certainly you should communicate with your spouse about how he or she makes you feel, but your spouse may not be able to give you exactly what you want right away. Sometimes you are going to have to choose to keep acting upon the truth even when you are in pain.

Third, share your fear with your spouse and make a commitment to more open communication. Fears we keep bottled up inside usually cause us more harm than those which we talk through with our spouse. I've asked men to share their fears with their wives in the process of marriage counseling. They commonly say things like: "I'm afraid you'll attack me," or "I wonder if you'll be ashamed of me." Yet, it's amazing what usually happens when these fears are shared. Sometimes tears fall; sometimes a hand reaches out to express support. Most often, acceptance is offered.

You may find that simply telling your spouse, "I'm afraid you won't accept me if I open up," allows your partner a chance to share similar fears. This is a relatively non-threatening way to open some doors. Fear often immobilizes a person, but action tends to dispel fear. This one positive action may be the first step in successfully dealing with fear of intimacy.

As you share your feelings, commit to maintaining open communication. You may wish to say to each other, "It doesn't always feel good and it may be difficult to follow through, but we'll begin to take more risks in our marriage. We will begin to be more open in what we say and how we say it."

Finally, personal prayer helps overcome the fear of intimacy. When Paul told Timothy "God has not given us a spirit of timidity" (2 Timothy 1:7), he was reminding Timothy that fear must never obscure God's purposes in our lives. Intimacy is one of God's purposes in marriage. Since you know intimacy is God's purpose, and you know God doesn't intend to have fear rob you of his purpose, pray!

Ask God to help you replace fear with peace. Ask him to help you tell yourself the truth and to act upon the truth. Finally, spend enough time in God's presence so that fear can be erased. Remember the psalmist who walked through many valleys and concluded, "I will trust in thee and not be afraid."

Embracing Intimacy

Take a few moments to consider what you want — both as an individual and as a couple. If you long for closeness and acceptance, ask yourself what it is that inhibits you from achieving it. Is your prayer journey hampered by fear? What goes on inside you when you think about becoming emotionally or spiritually close to your spouse? How easy has it been for you to admit when you've been wrong, and to ask forgiveness? How do you feel when you think of sharing a secret with your spouse? Can you express your feelings with your mate, both positive and negative?

Feel free to set this book aside and think about those questions. When you are finished, try to pin down one thing you can do in your marriage that will begin to dispel fear, and in turn foster a new level of intimacy.

Overcoming the fear of intimacy is too vast a topic to cover fully in this book. But you need to understand that if a long-standing or severe problem exists in your marriage, you would be wise to seek counseling. A counselor can guide you through the healing process with trained supervision and encouragement.

Together with Our First Love

Perhaps the most basic aspect of prayer is sharing our lives with God. This personal relationship with our First Love encompasses all our attitudes, emotions, and thoughts. When we share this prayer relationship as a couple, intimacy can be measured, not with a teaspoon — but with a shovel! Praying together increases the intimacy in our marriage, but something even more vital occurs — we get to know God better. Sometimes we forget that the essence of prayer is friendship with God.

So prayer doesn't need to be approached as if it were, say, an encounter with Queen Elizabeth. In such a formal situation, most of us would worry about how to speak, what to do — we would be entirely *self*-conscious. Prayer, by contrast, is the practice of being *God*-conscious. More than anything else, it resembles the interaction between close friends. James Houston actually defines prayer in terms of relationship: "Prayer is the choice to direct ourselves towards God's friendship, to reach beyond human relationship to the love of God."[6]

Houston goes on to describe all of prayer as friendship with God, a friendship that radically changes our lives. Yes, prayer is communication with God, but more than anything else, true prayer is the pursuit of intimate friendship with God.

Listen with Your Heart

When we think of prayer as a way to express our needs, we often forget an important aspect of prayer: listening. Listening prayer is what happens when couples pause to experience God's presence, to listen to his still small voice, and to simply be with him.

Why is listening so important? Any good relationship needs effective communication to grow. This kind of communication requires our ability to express ourselves as well as actively listen to another person. Listening to God is part of developing spiritual intimacy. It's imperative to our relationship with God. To neglect listening will diminish our intimacy with God.

This intimate relationship has been practiced by believers throughout the ages, ordinary people who approached prayer as a means of carrying on a continuing conversation with God. It began with Adam and Eve, who walked and talked with God in the Garden of Eden, and has continued on into the end of the twentieth century, where the dear old couple across the street still walk through their flower garden and converse with God. Communion like this has nothing to do with a technique or religious exercise; it has everything to do with relationship.

One such person, who has made an impact on generations of believers, is Brother Lawrence, author of *The Practice of the Presence of God.* Throughout all the activities of a day, Brother Lawrence's goal was to develop and enjoy an awareness of God's presence. What a revelation! Though his life was a busy one, he sought and found God in the middle of whatever he was doing. "There is no mode of life in the world more pleasing and more full of delight than continual conversation with God," he wrote.[7] His life proved it.

Thomas à Kempis, a fifteenth-century monk and writer, prayed simply, "O Lord Jesus Christ, spouse of my soul, lover of purity, Lord of creation, give me wings that I may fly to you."[8] More than anything, his prayer was a joyous acknowledgment of his need for God and his desire to be in communion with him. We can all benefit by embracing this attitude: "Give me wings that I might fly to you." Whether prayer is breathed out during the high energy foot-race of life or poured out in the quiet of early morning devotions, communion with God is at its heart.

This may be a new thought to you. If you aren't comfortable with the idea, don't worry. We'll discuss it in more detail in chapter 10. For now, simply realize that prayer is more than asking!

Jesus' Words on Prayer

In Matthew 6:7, Jesus teaches us how *not* to pray. The methods he warns against would prevent us from achieving a real relationship with God. "Do not keep on babbling," he says. "Babblers think that they'll be heard because they overwhelm God with many words. The more words, the better." Jesus doesn't just warn us about repetition, but also about empty or mechanical repetition. Jesus reminds us not to treat prayer like a religious exercise. It makes no difference whether or not one's mouth is moving; if the mind isn't engaged, a person isn't praying!

Jesus told us not to treat prayer like a daily chore with an attitude of, "If I do this, my obligation to God is over." Prayer isn't a religious exercise! When prayer becomes automatic, it has nothing to do with relationship.

Jesus went on to say in Matthew 6:8, "Do not be like them, for your Father knows what you need before you ask him." We have a Father who knows our needs, who cares for us. So if the Father knows what we need, why pray? Because prayer has more to do with relationship than with relaying information. A. W. Tozer expressed it this way:

> God is a Person, and in the deep of his mighty nature He thinks, wills, enjoys, feels, loves, desires and suffers as any other person may. In making Himself known to us He stays by the familiar pattern of personality. He communicates with us through the avenues of our minds, our will and our emotions. The continuous and unembarrassed interchange of love and thought between God and the soul of the redeemed man is the throbbing heart of New Testament religion.[9]

Prayer is the continuation of a friendship — the deepening of a relationship with God. When we grasp this fact, we begin to change our view of prayer.

I remember holding my son on my lap when he was a preschooler. His three-year-old smile and his desire just to sit and cuddle with me were so refreshing. We communicated! Many times, there were no requests. And none was needed. We simply enjoyed one another. There are times in prayer when we simply sit on our Father's lap, wanting nothing more than his presence.

Prayer is as multi-dimensional as any relationship. It is varied, free, and flexible. It meets the needs of the moment. Prayer sometimes is as hard-driving as a jack-hammer, but may be as gentle as a child' s kiss. As you read the chapters ahead, remember that praying together creates a three-way relationship. As you pray, seek God himself, not material benefits. Perhaps that's the best way you can prepare for prayer.

How Deep Can We Get?

Praying for Aunt Mary who broke her leg and lives 2,000 miles away is one thing. Praying for your feelings of inadequacy on the job is quite another. Yet it's our disturbing feelings and mind tussles that most need the support of partnered prayers. The ability to pour out what's going on inside us varies with personalities, backgrounds, and circumstances. As you tackle the following questions, don't feel like you have to answer them all, but try and push past your immediate comfort zone.

Where We're At (both answer)

1. Your partner undoubtedly knows whether sharing is easy or hard for you, but try and tell them one reason why?

Prompter: What's your comfort level? Do you like to analyze or think about your feelings?

2. Look back into your past, share one thing that your parents conveyed to you about yourself that really affected you.

Prompter: Loved/accepted — or not? How they measured you?

3. What kinds of circumstances would be hard for you to talk about?

Prompter: Someone's death, sexual temptations, job problems....

A Step Forward

Having looked at some of the things in your life that make spiritual intimacy a challenge, name one area that you will work on developing in your sharing.

"Closet" Action

Take your partner's hand to pray. If it feels awkward, give yourself a chance to get used to it. Touch is a wonderful communicator. Now take your issues that make sharing difficult to God. Ask him for help in the area you want to work on.

CHAPTER THREE

Pray As You Can, Not As You Can't

This, then, is how you should pray...
MATTHEW 6:9a

DOUG AND SHELLY, a young couple who were about to be married, met with me recently to discuss how to make Christ the center of their new home. As part of that process, I encouraged them to begin to pray together. Both were new Christians, both loved God, but there was some hesitation, especially on Doug's part. After discussing their reluctance, a central problem emerged: They didn't have a pattern for prayer firmly in mind. "What do we pray?" they asked. "How do we begin?"

Sometimes couples are stymied about praying together simply because they don't know how. New Christians in particular may not have a well-developed personal prayer time, and the idea of praying with their spouse can seem even more confusing. Even those who have been Christians for some time may not have developed a prayer life together because they aren't sure about the mechanics of praying as a couple.

Relax! Don't feel you must duplicate a particular experience, as if there is some pattern cut in stone that must be followed at all times. Remember, prayer is friendship with God. With that in mind, just get your feet wet. You'll find that once you start praying together, talking with God will come naturally. Pray as you can, not as you can't!

If you don't have much experience with prayer, the following ideas may help you get started praying with the one you love.

Conversational Prayer

One approach that works well for many couples is often called "conversational prayer." This is when a group (or in this case, a couple) prays informally, with no set pattern. Think of how a conversation naturally progresses among three or four people. Those present speak whenever something occurs to them. Often, what one says sparks a thought in another. There is no leader saying, "Okay, now it's time for you to speak."

There are no hard, fast rules for a conversation — no special way to speak. When friends get together, they don't talk formally with lofty phrases or hushed tones; speech is relaxed and comfortable. That's exactly how a conversation with our Savior should be.

Adapting to conversational prayer may be difficult at first, especially if we come from a more formal church tradition. But consider this: If we can break loose from thinking about how praying should be done, we'll be more free to concentrate on God and our spouse — remember the threefold cord that is formed in marriage. Honest and heartfelt communication within the relationship is worth a lot more than eloquent speech.

Conversational prayer with your spouse can be exciting. At times, one partner will emphasize and perhaps further develop what the other has already prayed for. At other times, a spouse's prayer will bring to mind a different important issue. Sometimes couples will spend time quietly listening to God, allowing his voice to speak to their hearts. But just as in any conversation, there may be times when one spouse will have more to say than the other. That's okay.

When Naomi and I pray together, we begin by being silent as we become aware of God's presence. When it seems right, one of us begins. From then on, we simply pray as we feel the desire. We don't take turns necessarily. If you measured the amount of time each of us talked, it would vary, but in the long run it probably evens out.

Allow your prayer time to flow naturally. You'll find that you gain confidence as you go. And as you become more comfortable with conversational prayer, you can give each other support as you forge your prayer life together.

Praying Out Loud

Some people are not comfortable with praying out loud. And some of us are more than uncomfortable — we're downright afraid! This may stem from a fear of intimacy — that sense of anxiety that comes when we're faced with self-disclosure. To pray out loud, after all, is to risk exposure. It's also possible that we're simply nervous about trying something new. Maybe we don't communicate well. Or maybe we're just uncomfortable with the sound of our own voice.

One way to overcome some of these feelings is to pray out loud in other settings, such as during your private prayer time, or by saying grace at meals. However, discussing these fears with your spouse might be even more helpful. We need to share how we feel, and ask for support. Finally, we face and conquer our fears by actually praying out loud.

If your spouse is uncomfortable with praying out loud, you may consider that God has given you a special commission. Your love and acceptance can help create a safe environment for your loved one — a haven where he or she will not be evaluated or judged.

Pray in Comfort

One final word on the mechanics of praying together. Couples come from different backgrounds and often differ in opinion about the physical posture that is best for prayer. Should we kneel? Should we stand? Should we sit? The Bible doesn't specify a preferred position for prayer. Whether we kneel, as Jesus did in the Garden of Gethsemane; stand, as Paul did in a Jewish synagogue; or recline, as the disciples did at the Last Supper, our prayers should center on the attitude of the *heart*, not the body!

Most often Naomi and I sit in comfortable chairs in our family room as we pray together. However, we vary this from time to time. Sometimes one or both of us kneel. On occasion, we stand. The big issue is that the posture should not detract from centering upon God. If a two-hundred-pound man has to spend thirty minutes on his knees, he and his wife may find it difficult to develop a habit of praying together!

Creating a Structure for Prayer

Doug and Shelly, who were introduced at the start of the chapter, not only needed help with the mechanics of prayer, they also lacked a foundational structure, a basic pattern, to help them organize their prayer life together. Unless a basic pattern is established, couples often flounder in their attempts to become consistent. Many don't know where to begin or how to keep going. Once a pattern is established, a couple can become more flexible. We already agree that prayer is based on a relationship with God, and because of that no one pattern is absolute. But a basic pattern is helpful as a starting place.

Utilizing Prayer Laps

There are many themes that can make up a basic prayer pattern. One way to use your pattern is to think of each theme as a "prayer lap." For instance, to run a mile around a standard track, we have to take four laps. We can tell how far we've run by how many laps we've completed. To "run a lap" in prayer terms is to complete a certain theme in our prayer time before we move on. This breaks up our time into smaller units or "laps." You can easily keep these laps in mind as you pray, and it provides a helpful reminder for where you're going and where you've been. As a result you feel more relaxed and comfortable. You'll appreciate this even more when you're just beginning to pray together.

Prayer Lap Themes

Many authors have identified what they consider to be important "laps" in prayer. O. Hallesby identifies five elements of prayer.[1] Dick Eastman recognizes twelve parts.[2] Judson Cornwall, in his wonderful book *The Secret of Personal Prayer,* identifies nine channels through which prayer can flow.[3]

These writers all have slightly different ideas about what each "prayer lap" should include, but most agree on these four basic elements: praise, intercession, petition, and confession.

In fact, these are the elements that Jesus showed us in Matthew 6:9-13. When his disciples questioned him: "How do we pray?" his response laid out a practical pattern that can be used again and again. Each "lap" or theme of prayer outlined below is based on this prayer, as well as other Scripture. The last two themes — resisting and listening — may not be part of every prayer session, but they have value and need to be considered as optional prayer laps.

"Prayer Lap" Explanation

Praise: Thanksgiving, adoration, praise

Intercession: Praying for others — family, church, friends, and nation

Petition: Praying for our own physical, emotional, psychological, and spiritual needs

Confessing/Releasing: Confession of our sins and releasing others who have offended us

Resisting: Dependence upon God in resisting the evil one

Listening: Includes listening, waiting, receiving, submission, and communication

Jesus showed his disciples these general categories and expected them to fill in the details. He gave us a pattern for prayer. Naomi and I use this pattern in our prayers together. Because prayer is a dynamic, changing fellowship with God, we don't hold rigidly to the pattern. But it does provide a solid foundation, even when we decide to move in a different direction.

The Pattern of Prayer

You may be thinking: What about Jesus' warning not to participate in the kind of prayer that's just religious exercise? You're right, we don't want to turn this pattern into a formula to be relied on in lieu of relationship. But this pattern isn't meant to be merely a technique. It's a starting point for couples desiring to deepen their relationship with God. When you pray as a couple, I encourage you to start with these first four prayer laps and see how it goes. Feel free to make the last two laps optional, according to your needs. Remember, the most important thing is to just do it!

Praise

In Matthew 6:9 Jesus begins our pattern with an emphasis on praise that grows out of an intimate relationship. Notice how this prayer starts: "Our Father." We're not praying to some dignitary before whom we must grovel, nor do we pray to some cosmic superman far above us. We're coming to the God who calls us his children. Our Father, who continually overwhelms our souls with good gifts. How can we not praise him?

Naomi and I always begin our prayers together with praise, recognizing and thanking God for who he is and what he has done. We think of the previous day and thank God specifically for his good gifts that day. We then meditate on some attribute of God that we've seen at work in our lives and praise him for it. Sometimes we sing a chorus or hymn that praises God.

There are countless ways to praise God. Some couples choose a psalm of praise and read it back to God, personalizing it by using their own names.

Near our wedding anniversary, Naomi and I decided to remember as many times as we could when we'd seen God's love in our marriage, and then praise and thank him for each of those good gifts. Forty-five minutes later, a flood of gratitude and well-being overflowed our hearts.

Sometimes, unexpected ways of praising God appear. One beautiful day last summer, Naomi and I decided to pray in our heavily wooded backyard. I wanted to begin with praise, but I was discouraged. I had heard some bad news over the previous two days. So I decided to pray with my eyes open. As I looked at those majestic evergreen trees and the immaculate beauty of the day, God seemed to be saying, "I have a plan. I am in control." God's creation pointed me to him, and praise was the natural result. I expressed my love for my Father who is sovereign, and who holds my future in his hands.

Allow prayer to happen naturally. Don't let the pressure of format keep you from praying.

As God's children, we invite his kingdom to come crashing into the situations around us.

Conversation with God is not to be a one-way event, but a two-way relationship.

The Scriptures offer many examples of different ways to worship. We can use our voices to sing, to shout, or to speak our praises to God. We can use our hands to clap, to raise up in praise, or to play instruments. We can use our bodies to stand in his presence or to bow or kneel. The way is not so important as the attitude that says, "I want to respond to my Father in love."

Praise consists of two elements: 1) thanking God for what he has done and 2) praising him for who he is. It's good for us to spend time with our spouse, recognizing the universe of blessings God has given us.

The writers of the Psalms were so varied in their praise; their example encourages us to be creative as well. At one time the psalmist may be overcome with the majesty of God: "O LORD my God, you are very great; you are clothed with splendor and majesty" (Psalms 104:1). At other times, a simple affirmation of love is enough: "I love you, O LORD, my strength" (Psalms 18:1).

What should be our first response to God in our relationship with him? Praise. "Hallowed be your name," we say. I like the Good News Bible's translation: "Our Father in heaven: May your holy name be honored." "Hallowed" means simply to treat as holy. Jesus is saying that prayer, communication with God, should begin with an honoring of who God is and what he has done. His name — and the person for whom that name stands — is holy. We are to acknowledge that in our prayer lives.

As we remember what God has done in our lives, we can't help but be comforted. Life's roller coaster ride can produce so much anxiety! But peace and trust is the result of a heart full of praise and thanksgiving. As Martin Luther said, "In 'thanksgiving' we recount blessings received and thus strengthen our confidence and enable ourselves to wait trustingly for what we pray."[4]

Intercession

Matthew 6:10 provides the second prayer lap for us to consider: interceding for God's will to be accomplished. Intercession is simply praying for the needs of others. However, Jesus asked us to think of this privilege in a certain way. Continuing with his lesson on prayer, Jesus asked us to pray, "Your kingdom come, your will be done on earth as it is in heaven." This statement contains an amazing fact: God wants us to participate in the rule of his kingdom on earth through our prayers of intercession.

A kingdom is a realm over which a king exerts control and authority. The kingdom of God is the realm in which God is in control. Think of it as God's will and authority. Jesus said in Matthew 12:28, "If I drive out demons by the Spirit of God, then the kingdom of God has come upon you." That is, God's will and authority have come upon you.

Jesus' prayer in Matthew 6 is an invitation for God's kingdom, his will and authority, to find expression in the here and now. In the original language, the verbs "come" and "be done" are found at the beginning of the sentence; this is a way to emphasize those verbs. Literally, the phrase might read, "Come, thy will! Be done!"

God is saying to his people, "You can have a hand in inviting my presence and authority into the situations in your life." Couples who pray together invite God's presence into their world. As God's children, we invite his kingdom to come crashing into our lives.

Almost twenty years ago, Naomi and I were involved in a faith ministry together with four other young adults. One of our members, Phil, fell off of a three-story roof. His back was injured and he suffered with back pain. Many people prayed for Phil, including our ministry group. Naomi and I also prayed as a couple, asking God to touch Phil's back. For months we prayed, sometimes laying our hands on Phil's back and inviting God's kingdom to rule. Gradually God healed Phil. To this day, he has no back problems.

Whether or not God brings physical healing is his decision. But notice how, in this situation, Naomi and I acted as God's agents of change, working as a team in prayer to invite God's will. We aren't to meander passively through life, but are to march straight ahead, inviting God's kingdom to rule over the world we live in. Jesus says, "Intercede for your world, invite God's kingdom to come crashing into the situations around you."

When Naomi and I come to this intercession lap, we ask God to accomplish his will in others. We ask him to meet the individual needs of the many people that come to mind. Often, we start with our own children, praying specifically for each child in light of their particular situations. Then we move on to pray for our church family. We pray for leaders in the church, and ask that the purposes of the church might be accomplished; we pray for specific ministries, individuals, and families within the church, and for unity in the church as a whole. There are always many who need God's kingdom to come crashing in! We often keep a prayer notebook to help us remember to watch for change.

We also pray for family and friends. Do you have a family member who doesn't know Christ? Intercede! Do you have a friend who is going through marriage difficulties? Intercede! At all times, the world about us needs God's love and grace and power to find expression in individual lives.

Of course, there are other ways to approach intercession. Richard J. Foster describes his way like this:

> After prayer for my immediate family, I wait quietly until individuals or situations spontaneously arise to my awareness. I then offer these to God, listening to see if any special discernment comes to guide the content of the prayer. Next I speak forth what seems most appropriate in full confidence that God hears and answers.[5]

One helpful aspect of Foster's approach is the way he links listening prayer to intercession. Instead of moving ahead with his own agenda, Foster emphasizes the importance of listening to God for guidance in his intercession. In the same way, when Naomi and I don't know how to pray, we pause and ask God to direct us. "How should we pray?" we ask, and then wait in his presence. Often a prayer direction will come.

In addition, Foster wisely counsels believers not to "shoulder the burden of prayer for everyone and everything." I second this advice. All of us would soon grow weary with such a burden, and it might cause us to give up altogether. If we pray for the same long list every day, prayer can become boring and meaningless.

Petition

Our third prayer lap is based on Matthew 6:11 — " Give us today our daily bread." After we've come to the Father in praise and we've invited his will to rule in the lives of others, we present our own needs — this is called *petition*. The Good News Bible says simply, "Give us today the food we need." This element of prayer doesn't release us from our own work, nor does it somehow help remind God of what he has already promised to do; it is a statement about our day-to-day dependence upon the Lord. God wants us to bring our concerns to him, realizing we can depend upon him.

"Our daily bread" is a basic request. Nothing is too big or too small to bring to God in prayer. Through the years, Naomi and I have prayed for things as small as help in preparing a meal for friends, to requests as large as expressing a need for physical or spiritual healing for our lives. God has heard each prayer. As Paul teaches, we can "approach God with freedom and confidence" (Ephesians 3:12), knowing that he wants to help us in our time of need.

Most couples need wisdom for the decisions they must make. Naomi and I have never made a major decision without praying together about it first and asking God to guide us. Even in less important decisions, we have the privilege of bringing our need to God. Recently, we prayed together about whether to home school our ten-year-old son. Following this request, we paused to listen for

God. It's not always easy to listen for God's will without allowing our own thoughts to intrude, but we tried to still our minds so that his voice could fill our hearts.

As I think back over our twenty years of prayer together, I realize how vital the prayer of petition has been for us. Job changes, financial and physical needs, transitions of all kinds, wisdom for decisions, a need for spiritual growth or insight — all these have been the subject of these requests.

When we come to this prayer lap, we simply wait a moment and allow our needs to surface. Then we offer them to God. It's at this time that we pray for each other as well. Sometimes we request specific prayers of each other. At other times, our prayers are completely spontaneous.

Our needs may be physical, mental, spiritual — it doesn't matter. When we have a need, we take it before God, and, in doing so, we express our dependence upon him.

Confessing/Releasing

Jesus instructed us in Matthew 6:12 to confess of our sins to God, and to release, or forgive those who have hurt us. Remember that your prayer laps should allow for flexibility. If your need for confession is urgent, make this lap at the beginning of your prayer time, even before your praise. You'll then be released to move ahead freely with God in your time of prayer.

Matthew 6:12 centers on relationships and how, if neglected, our lives can be hindered. Most important is our relationship to God, and he invites us to keep a clean slate with him at all times. Every time we approach God we need to confess and be truly sorry for our own sin: "Forgive us our debts."

If we attempt to hide a part of ourselves from God, we only alienate ourselves from him and put up a barrier. Prayer's not just a way of getting something from God — it's a means of furthering a friendship with him. A clear conscience is essential to good relationships. Paul said just that in Acts 24:16: "So I strive always to keep my conscious clear before God and man."

Some of us may find it difficult to confess to God in front of our spouse. That's understandable. We need to be careful with our level of transparency here. This isn't necessarily the right time to bear all to God. Couples experience different levels of intimacy at different times of their lives. How one confesses to God in the presence of his or her spouse must depend upon the depth of that intimacy. Even when couples are close, there are some things best left between an individual and God. For example, sins of thought — since they are between the believer and God alone — are sometimes best confessed privately.

Such concerns don't need to be a barrier to praying together. We can simply turn to our spouse and say, "Let's wait on God here and speak to him silently, then move on when we are done." This allows each partner to confess whatever is on his or her heart, without revealing something that might be inappropriate at that time. Do whatever is comfortable within your relationship, knowing that confession is an essential part of prayer.

God is also interested in our relationship with each other: "...as we also have forgiven our debtors." As you reach this part of your prayer time, the Holy Spirit may bring to mind some way in which your spouse has hurt you. Take the opportunity, perhaps through silent prayer, to release the debt and forgive. At other times, you may remember something you did that offended your spouse. Pause in your prayer, ask your spouse to forgive you, and then receive God's forgiveness.

Here's an example of how a spouse might pray: "God, please forgive me for the ways I ignored you yesterday. And Father, I confess to you the irritation and anger that rose up when Ron and I crossed each other. I confess that I've held on to that. But now I release Ron of the debt — I forgive him. Help me now to say and do the things that show him that forgiveness."

This element of prayer is one of the most spiritually healthy things we can do for ourselves — and the one we love. Guilt and unwillingness to forgive are two powerful emotions. Holding on to them brings great harm to our relationships. When we ask forgiveness for our sins and release others of their debts daily, we are set free.

Resisting

Matthew 6:13 makes the final point of this portion of text: dependence upon God in resisting the evil one. The verse reads, "Lead us not into temptation, but deliver us from the evil one."

The Greek word translated "temptation," *peirasmos,* can also mean "trial." Many commentators prefer this translation of the word in Matthew 6:13, including R. V. G. Tasker.[6] "Lead us not into trial" is a way of asking God to help believers avoid those situations that might result in spiritual failure.

Satan, not God, tempts us. My best understanding of this Scripture is this: "Do not allow us to enter into temptation through the trials in our lives — help us to resist the evil one so that these trials do not lead us into sin."

One scriptural support for this interpretation is found in the record of Christ's temptation (Matthew 4). He underwent severe physical, emotional, and spiritual trials in the wilderness. Satan's strategy was to capitalize on those trials and lead Jesus into sin. But Jesus resisted the evil one and provided a model for all believers.

Naomi and I pray for protection from Satan for our family, our church, and ourselves. At times, we ask the Lord to "bind" the devil. We also pray that God will demolish strongholds — areas of spiritual weakness — in the lives of many. Over the years we've learned to appreciate the power of prayer and of agreement within prayer. These concepts will be expanded on later in this book.

Listening Prayer

Finally, we come to listening prayer. This element of prayer is not found within the Matthew prayer pattern, but you will find it inferred throughout Scripture, and it's confirmed in the prayer lives of countless Christians. Listening prayer emphasizes the relationship aspect of prayer because it centers on being with God and hearing his voice.

Bill Hybels illustrates why listening prayer is so difficult for most people.[7] He uses the analogy of a car engine. At ten thousand revolutions per minute, that engine is producing at full power, full speed ahead. Most of us are living our lives at such speed, rushing from activity to activity.

At five hundred RPMs, the engine is idling. Hybels makes the point that most of the time, believers approach God at ten thousand RPMs. We are busy; we get our business done in prayer and move on to something else. But we are more likely to hear God's voice at five hundred RPMs, when we have quieted our hearts and minds.

Jesus spent all night in prayer before choosing his disciples (Luke 6:12–13). What did he do during that long night on a lonely mountainside? Surely he escaped the demands of business and quieted his heart before his Father. And just as surely, there was a renewal of the vibrant relationship between Father and Son. Jesus undoubtedly spent time listening to the Father's will concerning his choice of disciples. Listening prayer is becoming aware of God's presence and waiting for his divine whisper.

Conversation with God is not to be a one-way activity, but a two-way relationship. Addressing his heavenly Father, Brother Lawrence referred to listening prayer as a sensitivity to the "grace of your presence."[8]

If we spent several minutes on each prayer lap, we would pray for about thirty minutes. But bear in mind, prayer should not be so mechanical. Naomi and I often find ourselves lengthening one or more of these laps, and then spending less than five minutes on another. Sometimes we leave out a lap altogether. But for couples who are learning to pray together, this pattern makes a good starting block.

Beyond Requests

Whether it's a little girl folding her hands in Sunday school or a man bowing his head in a search of life's meaning, prayer begins by asking God for something. It's automatic. It's natural. But we've just learned prayer's potential goes far beyond a request list. Let's discuss the other elements like: praise, intercession, confessing/releasing, resisting, and listening. *(Choose one or two to start.)*

Where We're At *(both answer)*

1. The following statements are designed to represent different responses a reader might have to this chapter. Pick a sentence that

best describes your feelings and share with your spouse (or just say it in your own words).

• This type of prayer sounds so complicated. I don't even know what this chapter means by _____.

• This seems like a prayer formula. I'm not sure I can make it personal to me.

• I didn't realize there was so much to prayer, but I'd like to try more of its elements.

• I agree and relate to the way this chapter describes prayer and would like to implement these elements into my life.

2. If a specific "lap" bothered you more than the others, tell your spouse what it is and why it made you feel uneasy.

A Step Forward

Is there an aspect of prayer that you'd like to develop? Tell your spouse what it is and why it attracts you.

"Closet" Action

Try praying together by using each "lap" of prayer. If this bothers you, tell God why and ask for direction. Then use whatever aspect of prayer that attracts you both.

CHAPTER FOUR

Finding Time without Adding Pressure

Arise, come, my darling; my beautiful one, come with me.
SONG OF SONGS 2:13b

IF YOUR MARRIAGE IS LIKE SIXTY PERCENT of the marriages in America, both partners work, and you have two children. You deal with the pressure of balancing jobs, family, and church. It's a juggling act. Time seems to drain away each day like water on the desert. *Where did it go?* you wonder, as you prepare for another day. We are told to be "faithful in prayer" (Romans 12:12), yet you wonder how you'll ever get the dirty laundry done, much less consider the spiritual dimension of life. Pray together, you ask? You've got to be kidding!

Have you noticed that any worthwhile change in life always faces some resistance? Whenever you want to move in some positive direction, you automatically encounter obstacles. That's life! It doesn't matter that praying with your partner is spiritually beneficial. It's not exempt from the forces that resist change.

This chapter discusses ways to overcome perhaps the most common obstacle to praying with our spouse — time itself. Benjamin Franklin once said, "Time is the stuff which life is made of. To waste your time is to waste your life. To master your time is to control your life." The Bible talks about "making the most of your time" (Ephesians 5:16). But how do couples use time to their full advantage when it comes to fitting prayer into their already over-booked lives?

Allow Yourselves to Be in Process

As we talk about this issue of time, I can imagine your tension mounting. Many of us sincerely want to grow in this area, but can we really do it? Can we really give it our all? Richard Foster has excellent advice for us: "Let go of trying too hard to pray."[1] *What?* you wonder. *Isn't this exactly the opposite of what our goal should be?* Listen to Foster explain:

> Some people work at the business of praying with such intensity that they get spiritual indigestion. There is a principle of progression in the spiritual life. We do not take occasional joggers and put them in a marathon race, and we must not do that with prayer, either. If prayer is not a fixed habit with you, instead of starting with twelve hours of prayer-filled dialogue, single out a few moments and put all your energy into them.[2]

Foster's words apply well to couples. Life is a race with many challenging miles to run. Shoulds and oughts only add pressure to the race. When prayer becomes a burden, something is wrong. It may be that we aren't ready to do all that we desire to do. We must allow growth to progress over time.

We need to recognize where we are in our spiritual journey. We must do some honest evaluating. Foster's analogy of running is right on target. When we begin to jog, we mostly walk, then run a few yards here and there. Before long, we run part of the distance and walk the rest. Eventually we run the entire length of the course, and may even lengthen the distance as our physical conditioning progresses.

As couples, we need to ask ourselves where we are in our spiritual conditioning, and not place more pressure on ourselves than is sensible. High expectations are fine, but unrealistic expectations are a killer. One young couple told me they had no regular times of prayer. However, they did try to pray together as often as possible for at least a few minutes. Did I tell them they were failing? Absolutely not! This couple had evaluated their situation and were doing what they could. Naturally I would encourage any couple to take the next step of growth, but we also need to let go of killer expectations.

The emphasis of this book is on *praying together*, not spending a certain amount of time in prayer, or even praying together on a daily basis. Allow yourselves to be in process. Know what you are capable of doing and do it, but don't pressure yourselves to meet expectations that you cannot live up to.

Agree on Your Priorities

There is, of course, another side to the coin. Certainly, couples should not pressure themselves. They need to go at their own pace. Some seasons in life will force us to pray on the go. But if we're serious about growth, we should evaluate our lives and agree upon the priority of prayer. After going through the first few chapters of this book, I hope you agree that praying together can strengthen your marriage. However, it's one thing to *know* prayer will contribute to a relationship but quite another to consciously *commit* to make prayer a priority.

Management consultant Stephen R. Covey discusses the reasons for lack of effective time- and life-management in people's lives:

> Most people say their main fault is a lack of discipline. On deeper thought, I believe that is not the case. The basic problem is that their priorities have not become deeply planted in their hearts and minds.[3]

How committed are we to making prayer a priority that's implanted in our hearts and minds? We can agree that praying together is good, but are we ready to make it a vital part of our relationship? That takes commitment. And commitment is a word we usually don't take too lightly.

Paul Stevens, marriage counselor and author, tells the story of a young newlywed couple on their wedding night. The new bride stops her husband and says, "Aren't you going to pray?" The nonplused young husband drops to his knees and says, "Dear Lord, for what we are about to receive, make us truly thankful. Amen."[4]

High expectations are fine, but unrealistic expectations are a killer.

You don't have to let what has happened in the past determine what you will do in the future.

Like all friendships, prayer develops best through regular contact.

All joking aside, it's surprising how many Christian couples start their married lives with such confusion. The issue of prayer usually comes up sometime in the beginning of the marriage. Often some embarrassment and awkwardness is present. Who should take the lead? How do we do it? If a partner feels uncomfortable or has a bad experience, prayer may never get off the ground. Or if one partner is too forceful with a more reluctant mate, praying together can be colored by negative emotions. The end result can be that a couple may be married for years but never experience anything resembling a satisfying prayer life.

The good news is this: It's never too late! Communication is the most important antidote to a negative history. If you agree praying together is important, then it's worth discussing your past as a couple, and how it has affected your prayer life. Be honest with your spouse. Find a new beginning together. You don't have to let what has happened in the past determine what you'll do in the future. Overcome your clumsy beginning, and take action to make praying together a priority.

Change and commitment usually come only after one recognizes a deep need. Are you convinced of the powerful benefits of praying with your spouse? Do you want to make prayer a regular part of your lives? If you can answer yes to these questions, finding the time is much easier.

Finding Time

Recently, I talked with a couple about how their week had gone. The wife said, "You know, we had such a busy week that we just didn't have time to pray together." Naturally, I was sympathetic and didn't heap guilt on these new Christians. However, I gently asked one question designed to help them think about their use of time: "So you two were busy and didn't pray. May I ask if you watched any TV together?" They looked at each other and smiled. "I see your point," the wife said with a grin.

All of us have *some* discretionary time, time that is not committed to work or sleep. It may not be much, but we all have it. We can choose to invest some of that time in praying together. This may mean that the television goes on less often or that hobbies sit idle for a while. Don't get me wrong; I think recreation is important, but when discretionary time must be budgeted, prayer needs to be on the docket. So how can we best use our discretionary time?

Praying on the Go

My wife and I keep several thoughts in mind relating to this issue of time. First, *some* time is better than *no* time. Some weeks are particularly hectic. Late nights. Heavy responsibilities. But even if we only pray together one time some weeks, that time is worthwhile. Even when we can't have all the prayer we want, this doesn't stop us altogether.

We all need to abandon an "all or nothing" mentality when it comes to prayer time. If you miss a few days, that doesn't mean you've failed and it's time to give up. It simply means you need to come up with a creative way to see that you don't miss your next prayer time. If your schedule only permits one significant prayer time a week, then take it! Even if you pray for five minutes, you'll still experience some benefits of praying together. Some time is better than no time.

Younger couples find the time issue particularly difficult to resolve. I talked to a young couple recently who conceded that their lives were hectic. They *did* have a prayer life together but it was something at which they both had to work hard. This wife explained:

> We don't have "regular" prayer times. We pray just about every day, though. The reality is that we have four small children. My husband konks out at night long before I do. Sometimes we turn meals into an extended time of prayer. We grab the opportunities when they are there.

Obviously this is not ideal, but who ever said that life must always be ideal? Did you notice what this young wife said? "We grab the opportunities when they are there." Marriage has seasons. Those early seasons are often more hectic and allow for less prayer time together. But that doesn't mean we should give up on prayer. We may just have to be more spontaneous. Finding time may be difficult — particularly if you have children and/or you both work — but the more often you find the time, the more you'll feel the time is well spent. And before long, you'll both be looking for ways to pray together more often.

A wife in a blended family told me this: "We have a good prayer life together, but we tend to be more random. We might end up praying in the car, for example, because we drive a lot together." What? Is praying in the car allowed? You bet! Obviously, if that were the *only* venue for prayer, there might be some eventual dissatisfaction. But it's definitely a way to pray while on the go.

One couple had a unique problem. The wife told me she had a sleep disorder and if she remained still for very long, she went to sleep. She had to be finished with prayer in five to ten minutes. Talk about a time problem! Her solution? Since she needed to exercise every day, she prayed with her husband while exercising on her stationary bike.

A wife told me that she and her husband often pray spontaneously for a few minutes immediately after he comes home from work. Sometimes the kids are under foot. This couple's favorite (and sometimes *only*) private place to pray is in the bathroom! We must use the opportunities we have in the best way we can. Praying on the go essentially means to be creative and alert for those moments.

When we're in the time-crunch trenches, we need to make

prayer work as well as possible without adding guilt. It may mean praying on the go, but with some ingenuity and a commitment to praying together, it can happen.

Planning for Success

Allowing for different seasons and difficult logistics, Naomi and I have noticed that when we plan our prayer times, they tend to happen more consistently. Some couples may be happier with the more spontaneous approach, but many will benefit from a schedule. You've heard that statement, "Plan your work and work your plan." Praying together can benefit from such an approach.

Right now, Naomi and I pray several mornings during the week. During the school year, we pray from about 6:15 to 7:00. The alarm goes off, we get up, we pray. No angels wait by our bed to escort us to the family room. There's no "Hallelujah Chorus" ringing in our ears. But we've planned, and we work the plan. We're glad we do.

Several years ago I asked myself, "How are we doing as a couple?" At that time it seemed that Naomi and I needed longer periods of prayer, so we arranged our schedule to make this happen. We realized we had to be in bed by ten o'clock if we wanted to get up early enough to pray together. We have three children, so this sounded impossible. But for us, it was a must!

Each couple must decide on a plan that works for them. One couple I know prays spontaneously during the week but always plans an extended prayer time together on Saturday mornings. That schedule fits their lives and meets their needs. The key isn't to try to duplicate what someone else is doing, but to find a plan that fits your unique circumstances.

A Habit of Prayer

Naomi and I have found that an important part of making sure prayer happens is to keep it regular. That means not biting off more than we can chew. It might be nice to plan five hour-long prayer times every week, but it's unlikely to happen. If you're just starting out, I suggest that you agree to pray ten to twenty minutes, perhaps twice a week. If that seems like too much, plan on just five minutes of prayer, twice a week.

The actual amount of time spent praying isn't as important as having prayer become a *regular* part of your life. If you make times of prayer a habitual part of your lives — as regular as brushing your teeth or setting your alarm — it will become part of the fabric of your lives. Later, if God directs, you can increase your time together.

How do we make time? Consider these four questions:

1. How many times a week do we want to pray together?

2. How many minutes will we pray each time?

3. Do we need to rearrange our schedule to make this happen consistently?

4. What will we do to remind each other of our prayer times?

It may help to take out pencil and paper and brainstorm together on these questions. You may also want to consider whether you want to consider a specific prayer direction to help you get started. Be sure to ask God to help you fill in the blanks. When you reach some conclusions, agree together about how you will begin to implement the follow-up actions. It may help to jot down your prayer "dates" on your calendar.

Arranging your schedule to facilitate prayer may be one of the keys to making it happen. You've surely noticed how the downward pull in life is always constant? There's always too much to do and not enough time to do it. Without our focus and attention, things that are vital — but not necessarily urgent — often disintegrate. Unless firm decisions are made about a schedule, it's likely that nothing will happen. When you discuss the issue of time and make a commitment that's recorded on your calendar, your chance for success is greatly increased.

One last thought. Some couples say that they pray "as needed." They pray when a need arises or when they have a decision to make or when God seems to prompt them. Most couples can relate to this spontaneous approach, and it is a positive component of a couple's spiritual life. There may be times in our lives when this is all that happens. But just the same, I urge every couple to aim for a more regular prayer time. The more we rely on the "pray as needed" approach, the more we tend to look upon prayer as a spiritual vending machine — a method to use only when we need something. Remember, prayer is about our friendship with God, our relationship with our loving Father. And all friendships become stronger and more rewarding through regular contact and fellowship.

Prayer Partnering

This idea of planning regular prayer times may feel overwhelming. What some couples don't realize is that the opposite is just as true. When we *don't* pray together, we may feel an even stronger undercurrent of pressure and guilt. Yet if we keep making time to pray with our partner we will be refreshed and encouraged like never before.

For several years, my wife walked with a group of three friends. She would drag herself out of bed at 6:05 every morning to meet them. On many mornings, she didn't want to get up. In fact, she often would have given a lot to stay in bed! Only one thing motivated her to crawl out of bed and into her sweats to be ready on time: her friends were waiting.

A solid benefit of praying together is that you have a partner to help motivate you. If one of you is less inclined to pray, the other one will often be ready and waiting — especially if you've set aside a regular time. If my wife and her friends hadn't scheduled their exercise time, she could have said, "I don't have time to walk today." But the time was already set, and her friends held her accountable.

Many things try to get in the way of prayer. Those obstacles can look bigger than they actually are. An attitude that's helped me in many different situations is this: "Assume that it's possible and then find a way to make it happen." We must assume that praying together is possible. When that's our attitude, we look for all kinds of ways to make it happen.

This issue of time can be dealt with. Whether in the car, in the bathroom, or at the dinner table, we can find ways to use discretionary time without adding pressure to our already busy lives. Go at your own pace, but go!

Against the Clock

Making time to pray is a lot like making a budget. It's easier to talk about and plan than do in real life. Every thing from unscheduled doctor appointments to job deadlines hinder our good intentions to pray together. So what can be done to get reality and prayer plans together. Thinking through the following questions may help.

Where We're At (both answer)

1. How often do you pray with your spouse?

a) Next to never b) When there's a need or problem c) Frequent to daily

2. How would you describe your prayer times?

a) Planned b) Spontaneous c) Combination of both

3. If I had to rate praying with my partner on a one-to-ten family priority list, what number would it be?

4. Compare your rating with your spouse's. Are they alike, a little off, or as different as night and day?

Share what you think the comparison indicates about yourself. Your spouse. Your understanding of each other.

A Step Forward

Talk over a realistic prayer plan (how often, how long, when) that both of you are willing to do and be held accountable to.

"Closet" Action

Give God your good intentions and acknowledge that's what they are. Ask his Holy Spirit to remind, prod, and prompt you to make them a reality.

CHAPTER FIVE

Working with Our Differences

And fit in with each other, because of your common reverence for Christ.
EPHESIANS 5:21 (PHILLIPS)

AT A RECENT MARRIAGE RETREAT, a couple talked to me about a difference in their personalities that had created an obstacle to praying together. To me, it seemed like such a minor problem, and yet it had derailed their prayer life for years. After the seminar the wife said to me, "This retreat has given us hope. After all, this is only one obstacle — one difference — and you've reminded us that our differences don't need to become obstacles." This wife demonstrated a complete change in perspective: "It will never work" became "Our differences don't have to control our spiritual lives!"

If Only You Were More Like Me...

Differences in personality, preferences, and experience are inevitable in marriage. That's what makes marriage such a joy. Wouldn't it be boring if we were all the same? If husbands and wives were exactly alike, what would they offer to each other? Often the traits that attracted you to your spouse in the first place, were those very differences. It's also possible that the qualities you found so winsome at the beginning may frustrate you now. What's more, you may see these distinctions as serious obstacles to spiritual intimacy.

Before we talk about some of the common differences that can hamper prayer, I want to encourage you to look at this from a new angle. Sometimes we perceive our differences as a giant unscalable wall that separates us within our marriage. But the truth is, our differences need not pose this kind of stumbling block to our prayer life together. They can actually become stepping stones to marital unity — if we let them. The next three concepts can help us see our partners' differences in a new and encouraging way.

Completely Unique

First, we must remember that God is our Creator. Every person has a different physical structure, including a metabolic and neurological configuration that God has designed. Our families also constitute a tremendous force in shaping our personalities, yet God chooses the families in which we are raised.

Consider the numerous and varied life experiences that make each person unique. At the same time, we also have God's hand guiding us along, molding us into interesting individuals. Then on top of this, we are given special spiritual gifts by God.

When we recognize all that goes into making us who we are, we can begin to see our spouse, differences and all, as God's one-of-a-kind creation — a beautiful gift to be treasured. In Psalms 139:14 the psalmist is moved to joy as he realizes that he is "fearfully and wonderfully made." So are we all! This psalm is an affirmation that "different" is not a synonym for "wrong" or "bad."

He's So Stubborn!

"Ah," you say, "but what about those truly irritating differences, the ones that are obviously problematic?" Of course there are personality traits which seem less than desirable. All of us see some unpleasant traits in our spouse, such as outbursts of anger or chronic lateness or passivity or impulsiveness. Such weaknesses can be quite distressing. But we can also see these traits with new eyes.

Negative traits are usually positive traits that have been distorted or turned inside-out. After all, each of us has a fallen nature which is subject to sin. There are no perfect people. What God intended to be a strength can become a weakness when we make poor choices. Consider someone who is impulsive and may even appear thoughtless. Take a closer look and you'll probably see a person who can be delightfully spontaneous. Spontaneity is the positive trait; impulsiveness is the negative. What about the person who seems unbendingly stubborn? That person may also possess the traits of perseverance and loyalty. Stubbornness may be a misapplication of those positive traits. A person we call a tightwad might also be financially prudent. Fiscal responsibility is the positive trait; being stingy is the distortion.

We must see our spouse's differences — even negative ones — as potentially enriching to our lives. This doesn't mean we should ignore traits that are ultimately destructive. Some differences are weaknesses that need to be dealt with. However, much of what is different in our spouse is not destructive; it is merely distinctly different from *us!*

Seeing differences in a new light is to understand that our spouse is God's creation, his gift to us. We can then concentrate on the positive side of each character trait and pray that God will show us how we can encourage our spouse to develop their strengths.

There Are Differences and There Are Differences

Remember, there are two kinds of differences: those that can be changed and those that can't. The latter includes things like looks, age, and body metabolism which affects how we get up in the morning and how high we want the thermostat set! Those things that *can* be changed include personal habits and preferences, such as whether or not we put the cap back on the toothpaste.

Differences that affect our prayer life come in both varieties. We need to understand that some differences will probably never change, while others are open to negotiation. As we learn to understand our spouse, we can focus on the positive side of their personality traits — and hope they'll do the same for us!

Responding to the One You Love

You've heard it said before: it's not so much what happens to you in life; it's how you respond that counts. This applies particularly well to the issue of differences. Our spouse's strengths and weaknesses are not our responsibility, but we are held accountable for the way we respond to them. Of course, God doesn't blame us if our spouse makes a poor choice, but he will ask about how we *responded.* Our Father longs for us to grow more like Christ in our attitudes and responses. Here are three areas of response to consider when facing your spouse's differences.

Accepting Our Differences

I am an extrovert. My wife, Naomi, is not. When I'm with a group of people, I'm energized. I'm great with small talk and meeting people. It doesn't phase me in the least. Naomi, on the other hand, is more subdued and has to work harder at new social situations. Not that she doesn't like people — she does. In fact, she has a wonderfully gracious and gentle heart — and most people love being around her.

This difference could have become a problem in our twenty years of marriage. I sometimes carry humor too far, or involve her in situations that she'd rather not be in. Sometimes I'm boisterous or spontaneous in a way that's just not her cup of tea.

What keeps this difference from becoming an obstacle in our relationship? Naomi accepts me — just as I am. Sure, she lets me know that she doesn't always track with my actions, but just the same she understands who I am and is willing to accept me. She communicates her acceptance in many ways — through her words, her attitudes, and her actions.

Of course, I've learned to be more sensitive to Naomi so that she isn't hurt, too. I've even learned there are times when I need to be calmer! However, her *response* to me has kept this trait from dividing us. Naomi demonstrates a key life principle: Acceptance is the soil of change. Just as flowers need soil to grow, so change needs acceptance to bloom. Accepting your spouse releases him or her to make changes that are needed, and affirms your mate as those changes are in process.

The first response to our spouse's differences must be acceptance. Acceptance doesn't always mean agreement, but when our spouses know they're loved and accepted, differences don't have to separate us.

Let's Talk

A second response to differences is simply to share our feelings with our spouse. Obviously, this works much better if we've assured them of our acceptance, no matter what. It's also helped by good timing — talking when we both can give our full attention to the discussion, and not when we are angry. A frank discussion of our differences and how they affect our lives should always open the door to understanding.

If your spouse is willing to listen and to discuss what's bothering you, share your thoughts and feelings in a way that's direct, but without casting blame. Explain that you understand and accept your loved one — that you're committed to him or her. This approach usually starts a productive discussion. Your spouse may admit that the difference is a weakness, or may not see it as a problem at all. The important thing is that you're talking with each other. And as I mentioned in an earlier chapter, your goal is not to change your spouse — that's God's job.

It's crucial that your spouse understands that you want to overcome any problems that these differences may have caused. You don't want to ignore the issue any longer. Your goal is to reach that place of spiritual and relational intimacy — together. This discussion, or series of discussions, can transform your relationship and help you to reaffirm your commitment to each other.

Give and Take

At some point, all marriages need a good compromise. There comes a time when we need to adjust our original preference in order to settle a difference. If we can bring up a problem and still maintain a spirit of acceptance, we may discover that compromise is the best result. There's something very sweet about making a joint sacrifice in your marriage, so that both of you can win.

What if you are very structured and organized and want to pray at the same time every morning, with little or no variation, but your spouse is more spontaneous and wants to pray when it seems appropriate, with no schedule at all? In a compromise, you might both agree to one or two scheduled prayer times a week with an openness to pray at other times on a spontaneous basis.

We need to celebrate our uniqueness! Instead of being put off by our differences, we can learn to accept, to compromise, and even to enjoy our individual natures in the way that God intended.

Praying Down the Wall

Finally, we need to respond to our differences with prayer. Without blame, we need to come together and invite God to tear down the walls that have been built from our misunderstanding of our differences. Each time we pray together, we cast away more and more stones that comprise the barrier that separates us. These stones have names like: "he's always judgmental" or "she's never reliable"— but as we lay them down, God can throw them as far away as the East is from the West. God invites us to be changed together in his presence. Does that mean he'll remove our differences? Never! Instead, he'll use our prayer time to develop our differing strengths — to foster unity. And as we learn to appreciate each other's unique style — especially in the area of prayer — our relationship will improve and grow stronger.

Overcoming Our Differences

Consider the differences which arise between you and your spouse when you pray together. You may be embarrassed to even admit these differences exist, or you may think you're the only ones whose prayers get sabotaged by the mundane or even petty problems that come up during prayer. Don't worry, you're not alone! Here's how some couples came to terms with some common differences that showed up in their prayer lives.

We Don't Pray the Same Way

A couple of years ago, Zack mentioned a difference to me that took me by surprise. He was used to praying forcefully and with energy. Sometimes he liked to stand and pace while praying. His wife was used to more contemplative prayer, with more time for pausing or listening. Instead of talking the issue out, they had simply become discouraged and given up on praying together. A difference in style had become an obstacle to prayer.

A woman told me about a style difference within her marriage that had bugged her for years: he was "long winded." Now don't laugh! I've heard other couples mention this difference, too. In this case, the husband would pray for minutes on end, not allowing his wife to slip in a word to God. This woman sincerely told me, "It's hard to agree in prayer with your partner when you've tuned him out!"

Both these couples resolved to accept one another's style and to blend the two together during prayer. How did this happen? Quite simply. Zack and his wife decided to encourage each other with room to pray in their own way. Instead of being irritated with the other's style, they tried to flow with it. Although Zack sometimes still dominates the three-way conversation, his wife has learned to accept it. Zack, on the other hand, has come to accept and expect times of quiet and reflection in their prayer time. At first he was somewhat uncomfortable with the pace. But before long he learned to listen to both God and his wife. And they eventually came to a place where they experienced the joy of agreeing in prayer. The long-winded husband in the second illustration finally learned to shorten his verbal volleys, allowing his wife a chance to become more involved. She had to retrain herself to listen to his petitions without tuning him out and before long, they too were agreeing in prayer!

Perhaps you've had trouble praying with your spouse because you don't seem to mesh in style. Why not discuss how you can find common ground that accepts and welcomes each other's unique style? After all, prayer is important enough to warrant change. Just talking about the situation could bring about some adjustments. If this is an issue for you, take the opportunity at the end of this chapter to talk with your spouse honestly.

I'm Not As Spiritual As You

Some couples report difficulty in praying together because one partner seems more spiritually advanced than the other. There are lots of reasons why this might be so. Perhaps one spouse accepted Christ much later than the other. Or maybe one has more spiritual interest and spends more time in study and prayer.

This may be true of your marriage. If so, your differences may eventually resolve themselves, but a number of problems could occur in the meantime. How you handle them will impact the way you interact as prayer partners. Does the more "advanced" partner send out subtle signals of impatience with the style or method of the other? Does the younger Christian feel defensive or proud, perhaps refusing to share his or her feelings? Maybe the partner with less spiritual experience says, "I don't know what to pray," or "I feel embarrassed," and stays quiet, unwilling to risk.

Let's not forget that we're all "heirs of the precious gifts of life," equal in personhood and in standing before God. No matter how far advanced one spouse may appear, we all come to God by the same grace. A new believer may have wonderful insights into the things of God, bringing a fresh perspective that the older believer needs to hear. Our measuring stick is not God's, and spirituality is not easily tallied. Remember how the Pharisees measured Jesus. We need to give grace and understanding to our partner as our prayer life develops. When we talk openly about our spirituality we welcome insight and healing to our relationship.

In addition, an appreciation for how prayer works might help you feel more comfortable about praying together. Once again, remember that it's *relationship,* not verbal proficiency or technical skill, that provides the key to prayer. Use this opportunity to discuss what the most meaningful aspects of prayer are to you.

I remember Dan and Lori. Lori was an active, growing Christian, and Dan felt inferior to her spiritually. Quite truthfully, Dan hadn't developed his relationship with God as much as his wife had hers. If Lori wanted to pray with him, he kept quiet and let her pray. He was too embarrassed to voice what was on his heart. As with many of the obstacles we've considered, simply discussing this issue made a big difference for them. Dan was able to tell Lori about his fear of praying out loud, and she was able to assure him of her respect. She honestly explained how much it would mean to her if they could pray together. It changed their lives and their marriage. It can change yours, too!

But I'm a Night Person

My wife, Naomi, is one of those people who come to life at 10:00 P.M. She may have had a long day, but somehow she has a burst of energy at night. On the other hand, she has a difficult time waking up in the morning. She's the kind of person who sets the snooze alarm and wants to let it erupt at least three times before she crawls out of the sack. I'm just the opposite. I like to set the clock for the exact time that I want to wake up. Then I get up immediately. But I *do* conk out at night after — you guessed it — about 10:00 P.M. This is one difference Naomi and I have had to work around our entire married life.

A number of couples have talked to me about this matter of differing internal clocks. Brenda told me recently, "My husband, Bob, is always asleep before I'm done at night." She typically wanted to stay up an hour longer than her husband.

Brenda and Bob discussed and tried a number of options before coming to grips with this problem. They agreed on a number of solutions. First, they usually try to pray as soon as Bob gets home from work. This isn't always convenient, but they use this time as often as possible. In addition, they plan a mid-morning Saturday prayer time that fits both their internal clocks.

Negative traits are usually positive traits that have been distorted or turned inside-out.

Acceptance is the soil of change.

We all have different gifts — we can either blend together like a professional symphony or clash like a junior high band.

Our internal time clocks shouldn't prevent us from establishing a prayer life together. After all, if we agree on the priority of prayer, anything is possible. Compromises can be made to recognize each other's preferences.

During our twenty years of marriage, Naomi and I have tackled this problem in a number of different ways. At times we have prayed early in the morning. When this is our schedule, we both have to be aware of what time we go to bed the night before. During times like these, Naomi sacrifices a bit more to make sure we pray together.

Since I have a flexible schedule, we sometimes pray together while I'm home for lunch. At these times, I sacrifice a bit more because it eats into my afternoon schedule. We both think the sacrifices are worth the benefits we gain from praying together.

Different Gifts for Different Lifts

Whether we recognize it or not, we all have spiritual gifts. These are the special abilities God gives each believer to help serve and build the Church. First Peter 4:10 underscores the purpose of these gifts: "Each one should use whatever gift he has received to serve others, faithfully administering God's grace in its various forms." When we use our spiritual gifts to build up others, we actually share God's grace with them.

There are a number of gifts listed in Romans 12:6–8, Ephesians 4:11, 1 Corinthians 12:8–10, and 1 Corinthians 12:28–30. These include teaching, encouragement, giving, mercy, faith, help, and administration. Imagine how a baseball team works together to win a game. There are many different positions, and all of them play an important part. A team may be great, but without a first baseman, they wouldn't get the job done. In the same way, the Church needs to have all the gifts in operation so that God's purpose can be accomplished. Each gift — and each person — is important.

I wanted to touch upon the importance of spiritual gifts because so often there's a built-in difference between partners and their gifts. Many husbands and wives have very different gifts. For years I've asked couples what their gifts are and am constantly amazed at the complementary nature of the mix. One spouse identifies "mercy and intercession" as his or her gifts and the other says, "prophet and teaching." A difference in gifts is quite common and, depending on how they're handled, can either blend like a professional symphony or clash like a grade school band.

God's gifts often bring along with them a certain point of view. We sometimes react to events and needs based on our spiritual gifts. Sandy told me that praying with her husband frustrated her until she realized how he prayed was influenced by his gifting. "I couldn't understand how Dwight prayed," she said. "It drove me crazy." After taking a course on spiritual gifts she was able to appreciate the differences and not react to them. She told me how this change happened:

> Dwight's gift is compassion. He prays from his feelings, not the facts. As he prayed, I'd be thinking, *That's not the solution.* Since I'm more analytical and operate more from my gift of administration, I'd be critical. Underneath my breath I'd be saying, "God, here's the real prayer solution." Lately, I've been learning to see things from Dwight's point of view and appreciate the gifts God gave him. I've begun to realize that we *can* agree in prayer when we intercede for someone; we just pray for different aspects of the same problem.

Perhaps you can relate to Sandy's observations. And if you learn to appreciate your spouse's distinct spiritual gifting and unique viewpoint, you can let go of a critical attitude and enjoy a fresh perspective that you might have missed otherwise. We can benefit from each other's unique gifts. These amazing gifts promise to color and enhance our prayer life in a fun and creative way. The same God who designed the giraffe and the elephant took the time to make us, and gift us, in a way that should never be boring!

That's the Way I Like It

One last area of difference comes in a package called "personal preferences." Any time we prefer one thing over another, we express a preference. Usually these preferences are small, learned behaviors which aren't all that significant; things such as preferring some foods, favoring a certain method of paying bills, or liking a neat environment.

Some of these preferences can cause difficulty in a couple's prayer life. If we grew up with certain religious training it can make a real difference in how we approach prayer as a couple. One wife told me recently that while she came from a Pentecostal background, her husband grew up in a Baptist church. Talk about different preferences!

A common personal preference is simply a particular method of praying. A wife told me recently that when she first became a Christian, she learned to pray using the acrostic, "ACTS" (adoration, confession, thanksgiving, supplication). "I like to go through the whole system," she told me. "When he plunges right into intercession, I don't feel as if I'm ready unless we've gone through the other steps."

Again, there's no right or wrong here; we're simply different. But if we can learn to accept our differences; to talk about ways we can change; and finally to compromise when necessary — we should be right on track for developing a prayer life that's vital and fulfilling.

A Positive Difference

If two people try and squeeze into a closet, you can bet an elbow will poke a rib, hair will flip your face, or some other "oops" will take place. Two different people filling one intimate space requires adjustment. Until you get situated, a lot of things stick out in the wrong places. But once you get turned around right, it's warm and cozy, not to mention comforting in the dark. Inviting someone into our prayer closet can be a similar experience. Let's look at how we need to turn to get comfortably situated.

Where We're At (both answer)

1. Now that you've prayed a few times together, what differences do you notice between you and your spouse?

Prompter: Length of prayers, what prayed for, emotions...

2. Honestly consider the differences you've mentioned. Do any of them make it hard for you to pray together? Share what it is that makes you feel uneasy and why.

Prompter: Mind wanders, feel left out, bored, confused...

A Step Forward

What's something specific that you or your spouse can do to help deal with these prayer differences?

Prompter: Shorter prayers, accepting each other's style...

"Closet" Action

Talk with God about your differences. Though they might need "fixing," be sure and give him the option to teach you through them.

CHAPTER SIX

Restoring Broken Relationships

*...go at once and make peace with your brother, and
then come back and offer your gift to God.*
MATTHEW 5:23–24 (TEV)

WE'VE ALL STRUGGLED WITH RELATIONSHIPS that are hard to hold together. But what do you do when the endangered relationship is the one with your spouse? Nothing is more painful than a broken relationship, especially a marriage. The good news is that God has the power to repair any relationship — our Father's delight is to reconcile. And one of the best remedies for reconciliation is praying together. It's also a powerful preventative against future brokenness. When we pray together we reduce the level of conflict and at the same time invite God's healing touch on old wounds.

The Tie That Binds

A woman once told me about the difficulties she and her husband had early in their marriage. "Prayer was an avenue in those early years

93

to bring us back together," she said. She described how praying about an issue with her husband often brought them to an agreement. Prayer made the difference in their relationship. It's difficult to remain stubborn or self-willed with a spouse when we pray together regularly.

Another wife described with great honesty her reluctance to pray with her husband when they had difficulties:

> I sometimes didn't want to go to prayer with my husband because it might mean that I would have to change, and conform to what God wanted. But *not* praying with my husband was worse, so I'd end up praying. God would usually end up changing my perspective!

Prayer changed this wife's heart. It helped her to be open to her husband and broke the barrier that had grown between them. Somehow, being together as a couple in the presence of God knocks down walls. It's easier to work together when we pray together.

Harmony or Discord

How can you have harmony if one of you plays off-key? And how do you know if you're the one off-key? Praying together promotes harmony. But just like an orchestra, it takes careful tuning and a lot of practice to create and nurture that harmony. In the presence of conflict, it's easy to seek something or someone to blame. Our spouses make easy targets, especially if they are partially responsible for the problem. We often point fingers at each other when there's discord. But when we pray together, the problem is perceived differently. Blame tends to be forgotten. As we pray, we tend to see our problem as something we're working together to settle. Our goal is to become tuned into each other and to produce a sweet sound unto God.

Matthew 18:20 suggests another reason prayer promotes harmony: "For where two or three come together in my name, there am I with them." When a married couple comes together in prayer, Jesus is present. There are no longer two, but three. What happens to conflict when both partners are aware of Jesus' presence and are willing to hear from him? It's difficult to maintain a hard heart toward your spouse in the presence of a holy God.

Prayer promotes harmony in yet another way. In Matthew 18:19 we read: "Again, I tell you that if two of you on earth agree about anything you ask for, it will be done for you by my Father in heaven." When we pray together with a desire to seek and do the will of the Father, we learn to agree in prayer. This form of agreement knits our hearts and souls together, and becomes a channel for submitting to God as a couple. Who's "right" about a particular conflict is no longer important. Our greater objective is to come before God as one.

My Way or the Higher Way

A husband told me about a potential opening he'd had for a new job. He was excited, thinking God had opened up a door of opportunity. But he and his wife had decided earlier in their marriage never to make a major decision unless they could agree about it. As they prayed together, he felt peace about the situation, but she didn't.

At first, he thought his wife was missing God's voice. Finally, as they prayed together one day, the husband heard something new. The Lord seemed to be telling him that he was working through the man's wife in this situation, and that the husband was to listen to her. The man turned the job down. Within one year, God confirmed that it was the right decision. Prayer became a channel for submission to God *as a couple*.

When Naomi and I pray about some decision that must be made, we will often turn to each other during or after our prayers and ask, "Did you hear anything?" We compare notes because we want to move in unity. Agreement is the key. We know that Jesus is there with us. We want to follow his voice, not our own. Within that process there is no room for personal agendas: We must listen to the Lord, agree with him, and pray in faith together. Decision making is made easier when couples look to God together.

By learning to agree in prayer about decisions, couples can begin to reach agreement in other areas of their lives. Agreeing with each other becomes natural. When there is a prayerful attitude, we begin to think in terms of Philippians 2:4: We "look out for one another's interests." We defer to one another. We pray about things we didn't used to pray about, so that agreement comes even more easily.

Cleaning the Slate

Every normal relationship goes through conflict, but in order to stay healthy we need to continually clear the air. Each time we come together in prayer, we get a new chance to come clean before God and each other. As we become more regular in our prayer times, we'll also become more aware of the need to keep short accounts. I agree with Gary Smalley: Most marriage problems are the result of accumulated offenses.[1] Over a period of time, more and more offenses mount up until a marriage hasn't got a chance. Regular prayer helps break this pattern of accumulated offenses.

Ephesians 4:26 states that we are not to allow "the sun to go down on our anger." That means we don't allow relational anger to fester, or continue for any significant length of time. Why? On the first day of an offense the wall between a couple is like papier-maché: easy to break through — not a major obstacle. The next day the studs go in; before long, the steel and concrete. Finally it becomes an almost impenetrable wall of emotional distance between husband and wife.

Praying together helps prevent these walls from ever being built. Matthew 5:23-24 shows you how:

> So if you are about to offer your gift to God at the altar and there you remember that your brother has something against you, leave your gift there in front of the altar, go at once and make peace with your brother, and then come back and offer your gift to God. (TEV)

Let's say you're about to pray with your spouse. You're about to come before the altar of God and give him your gifts of praise and adoration. You're about to spend time interceding. God says that the priority of relationship comes before the priority of worship and prayer! We can't have the privilege of a right relationship with God unless we're willing to have a right relationship with others. This principle must begin within our marriages.

One woman, married thirty years, told me that praying with her husband helps her confess when something is wrong. Her husband said something interesting in response:

> All I know is that there's such a freedom in prayer that we couldn't leave the unresolved issues unaddressed. Perhaps we prayed first, but by the time we were finished being in God's presence together, I knew we had to work something out. Conviction would grow, and I couldn't put it off.

When we make praying as a couple a part of our lives, we need to have a regular "altar check." Let's say you're about to pray. It becomes natural to say, "Is there something not right between us? Let's take care of it before we pray." Or when you've wronged your spouse in some way, you might have to say, "Before we pray today, I need to ask you to forgive me for…" When this attitude prevails, the slate is much easier to keep clean; no hidden agendas continue on and on; no hidden land mines threaten your every step.

When a couple comes before God on an ongoing basis and both partners are committed to being honest with God and with each other, there isn't room to hang on to anger. It must go. The relationship is blessed with a clean slate.

Breaking the Prayer Blockade

Even in the healthiest of marriages, a small problem — a harsh word or minor disagreement — can cause us to take a tiny step back from each other. Over a period of minutes or hours, this distance becomes uncomfortable. At that point, we can choose to do whatever it takes to move back to the center to repair the relationship. In good relationships, restoration will happen immediately.

For some couples, however, a different scenario is evident. Instead of routinely restoring the relationship, hurting spouses may take yet another step away from each other. Unfortunately, these marriages operate in an environment of emotional distance. And for these partners, the thought of praying together may seem impossible.

If prayer is to become a regular part of such a relationship, something must change. Two common problems keep us emotionally distant. If your relationship feels broken, consider how these two issues affect your marriage, and what changes may be necessary to bring healing.

When Forgiveness Is Absent

Do you know how it feels to make a mistake and apologize, but the person you've hurt refuses to forgive you? You feel trapped, shut out, or just plain hopeless. You may feel angry, too. Failure to forgive can destroy spiritual intimacy — and ultimately ruin a marriage. How can we repair the crippling effects of an unforgiving spirit in marriage?

Jean sat in my office some time ago and said to me, "Pastor Art, if things don't change, I'm divorcing him — I know it's wrong, but I don't care!" Jean had been married to Thomas for seventeen years, and they had been Christians for most of that time. Some time later, I met Thomas for coffee and asked him to consider meeting with Jean and me to discuss what was going on. He agreed. Six months later they began the process of reconciliation. The tension broke, and before long they both sensed new growth in their marriage.

How did this happen? Many factors were involved. But the bottom line is that Jean and Thomas responded to God — they were willing to change. One thing was absolutely crucial in turning the tide: forgiveness. Thomas was doing some destructive things in their relationship. He was withdrawing from her, not coming home from work, and staying away whenever he could. But this harmful behavior was partially a result of Jean's unwillingness to forgive Thomas for past wrongs. Consequently, much of their relationship was overshadowed by a critical attitude. Certainly Thomas was responsible for his actions, but Jean had unknowingly encouraged him to do the wrong thing.

Bitterness seals in destructive behavior. Think about it. Suppose a woman's husband isn't spending enough time with her. She's bitter, and reminds him of his lack of consideration as often as possible. In order to change, this man must admit he has been wrong. But what if she won't forgive? Who wants to be humiliated? Here's the rub, though: Refusing to forgive almost always guarantees the behavior will continue.

When we choose to forgive, the exact opposite happens. Our spouse feels supported, so instead of justifying wrong behavior, he or she can ponder choices without feeling threatened. God has a chance to work! We can try to change our spouse or we can allow God. Who is better qualified?

Of course, there are also consequences for those of us who refuse to forgive. These repercussions have to do with the nature of such an attitude. Unforgiving mates are prisoners — slaves to their bitterness. Let's say your spouse rejects you in some way. You're hurt, and with the hurt there's anger. You refuse to forgive, allowing yourself to become bitter. What happens? How do you sustain that bitterness? Simple. You decide to play the mental recording of the hurtful event over and over. Each time you do, you are rehurt. You keep the wound open and festering. As you mentally view that scene, you also provide commentary: "How dare they do that to me! Who do they think they are? I won't take it!" Refusing to forgive makes both you and your husband or wife miserable. It erects a serious barrier to praying together.

Perhaps you are in a marriage where your spouse continually offends. There seems to be no end to the hurts, no time to heal. This is a very difficult situation. We first have to recognize that God is with us in the midst of our problems, that he cares for us and promises to walk with us. Secondly, we must remember Matthew 18, in which Peter asks Jesus, "How many times should I forgive? As many as seven times?" Peter thought he was being magnanimous, but what did Jesus answer? "Seventy times seven." We must forgive as many times as it takes. This isn't strictly fair. After all, we're the one being hurt. But it is God's higher way. In the same way he forgives us, he calls us to forgive others.

A Special Case

Before I talk about how to forgive, one caveat is needed. I have occasionally helped couples in abusive marriages. Christian marriages are not immune from domestic violence. If you feel fear in a relationship, if you find that you are walking on eggshells to avoid your spouse's anger, abuse may be present. If your partner is physically harming you or physically intimidating you, then abuse is certainly present. If abuse is occurring, forgiveness is needed. However, accountability is needed as well.

What should accountability include? When I help a woman in an abusive situation, I ask her to clearly communicate to her husband that she will report physical violence of any kind to the police, should it occur. The spouse *must* know that consequences will follow. Secondly, unless the offending spouse is willing to enter a program of counseling to learn how to handle anger correctly, sadly, accountability may mean that separation is necessary. This may be the only action that will break the cycle of violence. Of course, the purpose of such separation is healing and reconciliation. But accountability must include a safe environment for each partner so that the marriage can become healthy.

Even though forgiveness is necessary, a wise handling of the problem is important. If you wonder about your relationship with your spouse, find a pastor or counselor who can help you evaluate the situation. Remember, not all pastors are trained in or aware of the issues of abuse. Well-meaning advice may leave room for the cycle of abuse to continue. Ask your pastor if he's aware of abuse issues and has experience in dealing with domestic violence. Be very specific. If you feel he lacks understanding, seek out a Christian counselor who can help you or refer you to someone else if needed.

For most couples, abuse is not a problem. However, other problems may have occurred to create a negative history. Forgiveness is needed to clean the slate. Without it, your prayer life together can't be liberated. Lewis B. Smedes sums it up so well: "To forgive is to set a prisoner free and discover that the prisoner was you."[2] Now, if you're ready to forgive, here's how.

Basics in Forgiveness

How many times I've heard these words: "I want to forgive, but what does that mean? I've said the words, but somehow it doesn't seem to make any difference. I still have the same feelings." It's a difficult dilemma and one that requires some thought. What does it mean, practically, to forgive your spouse?

1. Assess the debt. Sometimes a partner feels ripped off because he or she is asked to quickly forgive something as if it's no big deal. Start by assessing the debt. If you're having a difficult time, you might want to sit down and write out how your spouse has offended you and how it makes you feel. Some husbands and wives will be surprised to see they've run up quite a debt. Spend some time coming to the point where you know what you are forgiving.

Some may feel this is an unnecessary and even negative step. Why go over all that again? And for many, this won't be necessary.

But then there are others like Ann. Ann had tried to forgive her husband for years. She would say over and over again, "I forgive him, Lord," only to find herself in knots about it later. Jesus said we are to forgive others of their *debt* as he forgives us. Until Ann actually assessed the debt and really understood it, she didn't have a clear sense of what she was giving up to the Lord.

2. Forgive the debt. It can be extremely difficult to come to this point, because the hardest part of this process is making the choice to forgive. But if you want to be free, you must make this decision. When you are ready, take your list of debts, hold it up to God, and say, "Lord, you have forgiven me of a great debt; I now choose to forgive my fellow servant a debt." Then tear that list up. Get free! You thought you were the jailer, but you were really the prisoner.

It can be difficult to forgive some very hurtful experiences. You can't do it on your own, but only as the Holy Spirit helps you. The Bible is clear that the Holy Spirit is at work in you both to will and to work for God's good pleasure. He will strengthen you for what he has asked you to do. Use the faith that God's given you and make the decision: "Lord, I forgive." Don't wait until you feel like it. You've assessed the debt, now forgive it. Forgive as you have been forgiven.

3. Don't replay the hurt. You must make one more vital decision. Decide never again to replay the hurt in your mind. That mental recording wants to click on and replay. When you are tempted to relive the experience, mentally shout "No!" or "Stop!" Declare again, "I have forgiven my spouse, and I will not replay what is already forgiven." Then go on to turn that temptation into a prayer. Speak to God: "Lord, thank you that I have been forgiven such a great debt. Thank you for giving me strength to forgive those who have hurt me. Now, Lord, bless my husband (wife)."

If you are willing to follow this third step consistently, you'll experience something remarkable. Initially, you'll still feel pain when the hurtful experience comes to mind. As time passes, however, you'll enter a second phase of forgiveness: You'll be able to remember what happened, but you won't feel that knife stab of pain. You'll have experienced God's healing.

This is the step that most people don't take. They find themselves right back in the morass of pain and bitterness. A choice to forgive is a choice to guard your mind against the mental replaying of the hurt and all that such mental rehashing brings.

4. Continue to forgive. Of course, there are many ongoing issues in marriage which continue to bring offense or hurt. This scripture must become real in order for your marriage to realize its possibilities: "Above all, love each other deeply, because love covers over a multitude of sins" (1 Peter 4:8). This injunction is absolutely necessary when it comes to marriage because there will always be things in daily living that bring potential hurt. What happens when she comes across too abruptly in a conversation? What happens when he comes home late and has forgotten to call? What happens when an irritating habit persists? I'll tell you what happens: Your love must cover it.

This is true in good marriages as well as those that are hurting. My wife, Naomi, is about as pleasant a person as you're likely to meet. But years ago something happened that sounds silly now, but irritated me greatly at the time. When our kids were in diapers, Naomi had a habit of putting a dirty diaper in the toilet and leaving it. She would be busy at the time and would plan to come back later to take care of it.

The problem was that when I'd go into the bathroom, the toilet would be full of dirty diapers! Needless to say, I was frustrated by this habit, but it didn't change. Naomi was a busy mom, and she always had lots to do. So I covered the matter in love, cleaned up the diaper myself, and we laughed about it many times. Believe me, Naomi has covered many items for me as well!

It was a small problem, but life is full of small problems, small irritations. If mates don't have a spirit of love that's quick to cover faults and mistakes, then a marriage will always be in conflict. Small things need to be forgiven, covered in an ongoing way. If problems become serious, they need to be discussed and resolved. Ongoing forgiveness is essential in building a healthy marriage.

Ongoing Conflict

Discord constantly erupts in some marriages — seeming to lurk just beneath the surface. Such ongoing conflict can present a formidable roadblock to prayer and spiritual intimacy. If we can't get along, couples ask, how can we pray together? Husbands and wives can become so discouraged they give up, forgetting that with God, all things are possible.

I worked with Michael and Kathy several years ago. It was apparent almost from the beginning that they were quite different from each other. Michael was a man who liked to take the initiative. Results were the bottom line for him. Sometimes he was insensitive. Kathy, on the other hand, was relational. People were important to her. She was a good listener.

Michael and Kathy experienced a lot of conflict because they saw life differently. Michael would express an opinion about a mutual friend to Kathy. She would be taken aback by what she considered to be his callousness and would offer a different opinion. Tension mounted. Feelings of closeness decreased. Any activities that required intimacy were curtailed as the emotional and spiritual distance between Michael and Kathy increased. Of course, neither one felt like initiating prayer together!

Michael and Kathy needed to allow each other to be themselves. All of us can benefit from such an allowance. We must remember that feelings and opinions are part of the people we married.

It's difficult to maintain a hard heart toward a spouse in the presence of a holy God.

God says that the priority of relationship comes before the priority of worship and prayer.

Often the conflict cycle can be avoided if your spouse knows you are listening.

Think about your mate right now. Your spouse has a right to his or her feelings — feelings are a fact. If you find it difficult to accept your spouse's feelings or opinions, try something different. The next time your spouse offers an opinion or expresses a feeling about something, reach out, touch your loved one on the arm or shoulder, and say, "Thank you for sharing your feelings with me." If you want to then give your own feelings, fine; but don't do it with the attitude of an adversary.

What Michael and Kathy began to learn was that they were very different people. That difference became wonderful and exciting, not exasperating. They also learned to pray together even when there was some tension. The hurts and misunderstandings that come into most marriages can yield in the presence of a holy God. This matter can be taken simplistically, but the fact remains that when we commit to prayer in the midst of difficulties, our conversation with God gives him an opportunity to soften our hearts and give direction. When two people are willing to bow before God together, pride and resentment, plus the little knots of tension usually soften.

Some couples experience conflicts that are more serious than Michael and Kathy's. Anger and disagreement may explode frequently. For these couples, praying together is harder still because they must struggle with the emotional baggage they carry. Their situation is serious.

Conflict Resolution

Many books have been written on conflict resolution. Norm Wright's *Making Peace with Your Partner* is an excellent guide for couples who want to increase their ability to resolve conflict. Couples who want to improve in this area must learn at least three skills: 1) the ability to share feelings without laying blame; 2) the ability to ask for what they want without demand; and 3) the ability to actively listen to one's spouse, without judgment.

It is outside the scope of this book to explain these skills fully, but I'll briefly describe what I mean by each one. If you want to work on this area of your marriage, I encourage you to get more input. Sometimes it's difficult for couples to learn conflict resolution skills without a third party helping them. Seeking a counselor who can help you may protect your relationship from permanent injury. If you're just beginning to experience conflict, spending time with a skilled marriage counselor may be the best preventive medicine you can get.

Remember, there is hope. You can do positive things that will make your relationship better.

One of the biggest killers in a marriage is blame. This happens any time we make a comment that labels our spouse. Macho, insensitive, don't care, selfish; these are just a few of the labels we tend to give each other. Instead of labeling a behavior, we need to describe that behavior and the emotion it elicits.

If your spouse came home late one night without calling, you *could* say, "When you were so insensitive tonight and didn't call, you sure showed me you didn't care." Or you could say, "When you were late tonight and didn't call, I felt afraid and a little irritated." Which do you think would be more effective? This skill doesn't usually come naturally. We all need practice!

We need to communicate current needs. A husband or wife must be able to share in clear language what they need. We sometimes believe it's sinful to have needs or that asking for something we want is selfish. The result of this assumption is that we then often send indirect messages. Can our spouse read our mind? When a woman asks, "Did you see that new restaurant that went in on Main Street?" is her mate supposed to know she wants to go to there for dinner? A typical complaint might be, "He should know what I want." But how can our spouses know what we want if we don't tell them directly?

The best way to talk about a need is simply to state it as a request: "I need/would like, because…" How does that formula sound in practice? "It would mean a lot to me if you greeted me warmly when I come home at night because it makes me feel connected to you at the end of the day." Or, "I'd appreciate it if you left the television off during dinner because I like this to be a family time." If you need to, be prepared to go further by stating what you feel when this doesn't happen. "When I come home and you don't greet me warmly, I feel left out and uncared for."

Remember in the process to make a request, not a demand. People can get pretty stubborn when demands are placed on them. Proverbs 15:2 says that "The tongue of the wise commands knowledge." A request is more acceptable than a demand! A demand has a lot to do with attitude, that is, the *way* something is said rather than *what* exactly is said. But a demand usually sounds something like, "You're always late and I won't stand for it anymore. I want you to meet me on time!"

We need to listen actively. Couples often set off conflict simply because they don't listen to each other. One spouse brings up a topic. The other immediately tightens up or gets defensive. A cycle of blame and counter blame will prevent many couples from moving ahead. The simple skill of active listening can help couples break out of this destructive cycle.

The key to active listening is to listen in a new way to what your spouse is saying. You can demonstrate to your mate that you're listening by: 1) orienting your body toward them; 2) maintaining positive eye contact; 3) paraphrasing what you are hearing; and 4) always giving your spouse a chance to correct you if you're not hearing them correctly.

Orienting your body toward your spouse is simply a way of saying, "I'm here; I'm ready to listen." Sometimes we get used to speaking to each other from across the room, or even from different rooms! Look into your spouse's eyes and show your interest.

Then listen so carefully when your spouse speaks that you can easily paraphrase the message. You must listen for two things: 1) the main idea and 2) any emotion that is apparent in the message. Every message has these two components. Often the emotion is not heard accurately. Suppose a husband asks, "Is dinner ready yet?" The content is a simple question: Is dinner ready? However, if the wife hears impatience as the emotional component of the message, she might respond badly. Even though impatience may not have been intended, the damage is done.

Imagine a wife saying to her husband, "You left me out of the decision again! I had no idea you were going to buy the boat. You always do that! You've got to talk to me about these things!" This isn't a skillful approach, but if her husband will listen actively and avoid becoming defensive, he can begin a serious discussion.

This husband might respond: "What I hear you saying is that you feel angry with me about this. You don't feel included in decisions. You'd like me to talk to you ahead of time. Is that it?" When a spouse knows you're listening, often the conflict cycle can be avoided. You might be surprised at your partner's response when he or she perceives that you're truly listening.

Keep in mind, it usually takes several weeks to learn what I've just described. You may want to read a good book on this subject or get the input of a qualified counselor to help resolve your conflicts, but be encouraged. You *can* learn skills that will help you resolve conflict in your marriage.

Prayer in Process

Some couples think if there's any kind of sand in the machinery — any problems, any discord — they can't pray together. But if a couple can admit that they're in process, they can still choose to pray together.

Sometimes Christian couples feel so much shame about their conflicts that they feel like hypocrites if they pray together. That shame doesn't come from God. Admit you aren't perfect, continue working on the issues, and in the meantime, keep praying together!

Gary and Lois came from alcoholic backgrounds. They were new Christians who were trying with all their hearts to make their marriage work, but they were torn apart by conflict. They resolved to pray together, no matter what. Sometimes prayer was the only thing they had. I reminded them repeatedly that they needed to allow themselves to be in process. They kept praying despite their imperfect circumstances. Finally, they began to experience some of the benefits of their diligence. Prayer acted as a healing force in their marriage.

Prayer is not only a vital tool in keeping marriages strong and healthy, but it's just as important for avoiding conflict in the first place. If problems threaten your marriage, remember that if you both open your hearts and minds to God, he can help you to creatively solve them. If we believe it's possible to move through obstacles and improve relationships, we can then cooperate with God to see that improvement takes place.

Conflict in the Closet

One too many golf games, meetings or ? has been the hot topic of the day. One of you is tired of never leaving without a load of guilt. The other is fed up with the daily grind or dealing with the kids. Now, you're supposed to pray together! *Lord, fix my spouse!* What other options are there?

Where We're At (both answer)

1. In the midst of conflict, how do you handle praying together?

a) We ignore each other and no one dares to mention praying together

b) We try and shove the problem aside and just pray around it

c) We cool off and then try to use our prayer time to resolve our conflict

2. Speaking only for yourself, does this solution work? Why or why not?

3. Do you agree with your spouse's response? If not, why?

A Step Forward

Name a specific action you can take to help your spouse to pray when the day has been full of conflict. Then ask, "Would this help?"

"Closet" Action

Tell God the difficulties you have in talking to him when you're at odds with your spouse. Ask to learn how to be a better peacemaker. Or if you bury problems that sidetrack your heart from true prayer, ask God to give you the courage to deal with them.

CHAPTER SEVEN

Gaining Peace in Times of Crisis

Trust in him at all times, O people; pour out your hearts to him, for God is our refuge.

PSALMS 62:8

SOME YEARS AGO, I worked with a Christian couple in their thirties who lost their ten-year-old daughter to cancer. They were completely overcome with grief and pain. Sadly, they weren't able to pull through their crisis. Rather than move closer to each other and to God, they continued to distance themselves. Two years after the death of their daughter, they were divorced.

In marked contrast, I watched two other couples experience equally tragic circumstances. Both couples found a place of peace in the midst of the storm. The loss of a child is one of the most devastating traumas any couple can face, and both these couples experienced tremendous pain. Yet several years later they have solid, healthy marriages.

The difference in these three marriages was determined by each couple's ability to move together through the crisis, keeping God at the center. Many factors helped the last two couples, but a key one was their decision to maintain a unified prayer life. When the pain became overwhelming or when they needed help, they joined hands and prayed together. That prayer made all the difference.

The Chinese symbol for change is made up of two smaller symbols: one meaning "danger," the other meaning "opportunity." Every marriage experiences change points, transitions, challenges, and almost certainly some tragedies. A change point can either become an opportunity to move on and grow in Christ, or it can become a dangerous time that threatens the marriage.

When couples pray together, they help turn the danger of a crisis into an opportunity for growth. They help ensure that the difficulty will not pull them apart or rip them away from God.

Listen to what one young wife told me about praying with her husband during a difficult time: "It was so good to have a place to go with our pain. When our daughter was born prematurely, we committed to pray together about the problem. We were doing something positive rather than blaming each other."

Prayer often is the cement that holds a relationship together during such times. For Naomi and me, prayer has been the single most important reason we have been able to weather life's transitions and difficulties: when finances were a problem; when my father died; when our infant son died; when our strength seemed small and our hearts were discouraged. Through changes of all kinds, we have prayed.

What have we prayed? We have told God how we felt. We have asked him for wisdom to handle the situation. We have submitted ourselves to his hand. And in those times of prayer as we have held hands together, we knew we were there for each other and that God was there for both of us; and that was all that mattered.

When I went to seminary, we moved to the Portland, Oregon area, and I was without work for the first time in my life. When I did find work it was definitely a step backward! I was having great difficulty earning enough to support us. Every day Naomi and I would join hands and pray. In our bewilderment, we would simply affirm our trust in the Lord. Fear, frustration, and hope were all part of our prayer together. Naomi would pray for me: "God, give Art encouragement for this new day ahead. Provide for our family through him." I would often pray: "Father, I trust you to provide what we need." We would pour out our feelings to the Lord.

Sometimes when facing unemployment, husbands and wives point fingers at each other rather than take their concerns to God. For Naomi and me, praying together helped keep the focus where it needed to be. Emotionally, psychologically, and spiritually, the atmosphere would have been much less positive if we had not come together in prayer.

Other couples tell a similar story. One husband summed it up succinctly: "If we focus on each other during a problem, all we see are each other's shortcomings. But if we focus on Christ, we find a place to file the issue and be at peace while he works out the problem."

Have you ever met a couple who experienced a tragedy or crisis and instead of continuing in prayer, they slowly backed away from each other and God? Soon things fall apart. It doesn't have to be that way! Prayer can play a vital role in the process of moving us through crisis and change. Instead of growing further apart, a Christian couple can grow closer to God and to each other during such times.

Even when a husband and wife aren't experiencing a crisis, life is full of transitions. What about taking a new job? How about that move to a new state? How should we spend the money in savings? How can we *get* some money in savings? These are questions that couples can pray about, seeking answers from God. When that happens, couples not only hear from God but they also experience a greater confidence and unity about the answer.

Praying Through Tough Times

In order for us to know how to pray through crises, difficulties, and transitions in our lives, we need to understand the nature of prayer. Some couples believe there's some kind of magic prayer formula; that if they can just find the key, their crisis or problem will be solved. Finding "the answer" to a problem is not what we need most in times of trouble; staying close to the one who *has* the answers is essential. Maintaining a connection to our Father in heaven is all-important.

When we pray together, we help transform the danger of a crisis into an opportunity for growth.

We're all empty vessels in need of God, and therefore, in need of prayer.

Prayer — since it is an act of hope and trust — fosters peace in the midst of crisis.

When I lead a marriage retreat on prayer, there are always some who say afterwards, "We really didn't know what prayer was all about." Often, couples find it difficult to pray together during tough times because they misunderstand the nature of prayer.

We need to remember that prayer, since it's rooted in relationship, varies. The parent/child relationship offers a useful analogy. Children interact with their parents in different ways at different times. One moment they may pour out their hearts, sharing pain or happiness. Another time they may be listening to their parent's voice, learning to obey. Then there are those times when they may make a request, asking for something they need or want. In much the same way, prayer varies because it's a vehicle for communicating with our Father.

Leaning on Love

B. M. Palmer has called prayer, "the language of creaturely dependence upon God from whom our being itself is derived."[1] He means that when we pray, we express our dependence upon God. We acknowledge that God is the center, that we can't exist independently from God. Moses expressed a similar idea when he told the people of Israel, "The LORD is your life" (Deuteronomy 30:20). When we're facing crises or major decisions, taking time out together to pray reminds us of our dependence upon God.

In John 5, Jesus bracketed a long teaching with these words, "The Son can do nothing by himself" (John 5:19), and "By myself I can do nothing" (John 5:30). How can Jesus, who is fully God, be dependent? The basic meaning of the incarnation, after all, is that Jesus *is* God.

Notice, however, that Jesus calls himself, "the Son." This emphasized the relationship between himself and the Father, the interdependence of the Godhead. Since the Son had voluntarily "made himself nothing" (Philippians 2:7) and humbled himself as a man, he had voluntarily taken on limitations as the incarnate Christ.

Jesus exemplified this sense of dependence upon the Father in a practical way. Luke 6:12–13 describes the Lord spending all night in prayer before choosing the twelve disciples. Prayer followed by action is a wonderful picture of dependence upon God. This example still provides us with a model today.

Paul expressed his dependence upon God when he prayed for his "thorn in the flesh" to be removed. We don't know what this thorn was, but we do know it was a problem of some kind that caused Paul real pain. The Lord's message to Paul is significant: "My grace is sufficient for you, for my power is made perfect in weakness" (2 Corinthians 12:9). In context, the Greek word here might be defined as "God's enabling power." All believers need God's grace, his "enabling power"; we are dependent upon him. God left Paul a visible reminder of his dependence upon the Father.

How do we express our dependence? B. M. Palmer sums it up well: "This consciousness of dependence finds its only full expression in prayer; we lean upon God, and are at rest."[2] As couples, we go to God for our needs to be met. It is this acknowledgment of our dependence on God and desire to have a relationship with him that allows us to approach God in prayer.

Martin Luther, the brilliant German theologian whose intellectual powers, strength of personality, and prolific accomplishments can hardly be overstated, offered this prayer:

Behold, Lord, an empty vessel that needs to be filled. My Lord, fill it. I am weak in the faith; strengthen me. I am cold in love; warm me and make me fervent, that my love may go out to my neighbor. O Lord, help me. Strengthen my faith and trust in you. I am poor; you are rich. With me, there is an abundance of sin; in you is the fullness of righteousness. Therefore I will remain with you.[3]

We're all empty vessels in need of God, and therefore, in need of prayer. That is the very invitation that our Father gives us. Listen to Hebrews 4:14, 16:

Therefore, since we have a great high priest who has gone through the heavens, Jesus the Son of God, let us hold firmly to the faith we profess.... Let us then approach the throne of grace with confidence, so that we may receive mercy and find grace to help us in our time of need.

Demonstrating dependence upon God and the gift of his Son, we approach God with confidence. This confidence is not born out of our accomplishments, but out of confidence in what Christ has done for us.

We *need* our Lord: his guidance, his wisdom, his provision. We need to call out to him. Writes O. Hallesby, "Prayer and helplessness are inseparable."[4] Our dependence is total and drives us to prayer. When we call on God, he will answer with "great and unsearchable things you do not know" (Jeremiah 33:3). He will provide us with whatever we need.

Prayer always carries with it this aspect of dependence upon God. Not that God is wanting to put us in our place or subjugate us. After all, he made us in his image. He died for our sins. But only when we recognize our dependence upon God can we have a vital friendship with him. Only in dependence can we submit to him. Says Larry O. Richards, "Prayer, then, is the appeal of a child who recognizes his dependence."[5]

To weather the crises of life, couples must understand that they are dependent upon God, that he is their Source. Peace comes as we look to God for our answers. Together, we invite God into the circumstances of our lives. This sense of dependency allows us to rest in the arms of our Father, rather than pull away from our spouse when the tough times of life intrude.

Your Will Be Done

First John 5:14–15 reveals an important, related aspect of prayer:

> *This is the confidence we have in approaching God: that if we ask anything according to his will, he hears us. And if we know that he hears us — whatever we ask — we know that we have what we asked of him.*

When we submit to his will, God answers prayer. Thus, prayer is submission to God. Obviously, not everything we want is good for us, and if God granted every request, we'd surely get hurt. Plus, God's sovereign purposes would be thwarted. Think of how parents handle their children's requests. Good parents decide how to answer based on what's best for their children. In the same way, God does what's best for us, putting each request into the larger context of his will. We then submit to our Father's wisdom.

Jesus' experience on the Mount of Olives gives a clear example of submissive prayer. "Father, if you are willing, take this cup from me; yet not my will, but yours be done" (Luke 22:42). Jesus looked ahead and saw the spiritual, physical, and emotional suffering he would endure on the cross. He asked for another way. Yet his time of prayer was also a way to reconcile himself to God's will. Jesus prayed that the pain of the crucifixion be bypassed: The Father's answer was no. Jesus accepted this answer and poured out his life.

In John 8:29 Jesus said, "The one who sent me is with me; he has not left me alone, for I always do what pleases him." This is a picture of obedience and submission to the Father's will. Whether choosing his disciples, deciding about a Samaritan detour, or determining when to enter Jerusalem, Jesus' heart and mind were centered on the Father's will.

Into Your Hands

August 1981 found Naomi and me in a small storage room at a hospital. We had hurriedly pulled on hospital gowns and masks as we prepared to see our five-day-old son. He'd been born prematurely, with a number of serious problems. The doctors couldn't tell us if he would survive. We'd been visiting in Bellevue, Washington (our home was in Oregon), when Naomi went into labor. After David was born, he was immediately rushed to the University of Washington Hospital in Seattle.

We entered the neonatal care unit and saw several isolabs scattered throughout the room with personnel standing by, caring for their tiny patients. We went to David's isolab and slipped our hands through the ports on either side. Then Naomi and I laid our hands on David's tiny body, closed our eyes, and prayed. We kept praying, back and forth, until we'd spoken our deepest desires to God.

What do parents pray at such times? We prayed that God would heal David. We prayed that God would watch over him. We prayed that God would strengthen us and help us during those anxious hours of waiting. We prayed that God would help us hold onto our faith in him. Every day that week we visited David, praying for him, being with him. Although anxious, I knew God would heal David. I knew that our son would live.

A few days later we drove the six hours back to Parkdale, Oregon. As soon as we were settled, Naomi and I prayed together again. We felt the Lord's presence and knew he was with us. Not long afterward, the phone rang. It was someone from the hospital saying it didn't look good for little David. Emotion ripped through us like an electric current. We cried together, then once again joined hands. We waited on God, praying and listening. Somehow we were able to release David into God's hands. We told God we were willing to submit to his best for our son.

Within a few minutes the phone rang again. David had died, perhaps even as we prayed. Tears. Pain too deep for words advanced across our hearts and clutched deeply into our souls. We could do nothing but pray again, asking God to help us understand.

In the weeks and months that followed, our times of prayer kept us close to our Father and close to each other. We hung on to our Lord through prayer, and slowly, over the ensuing months and years, we found healing. The crux of that healing had to do with learning to trust God at a new level, learning to submit to his will.

You see, we must be willing to submit to the loving wisdom of an almighty God.

A Time to Wait

All of us must eventually face the issue of "unanswered" prayer. We pray and our prayers appear to be ignored. Suffering of some kind is usually the result. Sometimes we pray all the more earnestly, trying at all costs to convince God of the validity of our petition. Still nothing happens.

The questions these situations bring to the surface are not easily answered. But there are important truths to keep in mind. God answers every prayer in one of three ways: yes, no, or wait. Sometimes we ask for things that aren't truly good for us. On those occasions, God must say no. Naomi and I have no way of knowing how healthy David would have been had he lived. Perhaps his death was part of God's mercy. We don't know. We only know that God knows best.

The apostle Paul prayed for the "thorn in the flesh" to be taken from him. God's answer was no (2 Corinthians 12:7–10), perhaps for a different reason. Paul's "unanswered prayer" may have fit into a higher purpose that God had for him: perhaps this was a way to help Paul depend entirely upon his Father. Sometimes, no is the best answer for us because it produces an eternal result somewhere in the human heart.

Hundreds of years before Paul, Moses prayed that God would take Israel out of bondage. For him, the answer from God was wait. God first wished to demonstrate his power through the ten plagues (Exodus 5-6). God's timing is often a factor in "unanswered prayer." Sometimes he must bring circumstances into alignment so that his will can be accomplished. Being impatient creatures, we don't like delays, but they are at times God's best answer for us.

Richard Foster suggests that sin sometimes hinders our prayers from being answered as well. He doesn't intimate that we need some special holiness before God hears our prayers. Instead he says:

> Sin, by its very nature, separates us from God, rupturing the intimate fellowship and dulling our spiritual sensitivities. We become nearsighted and develop thickened eardrums, if you will. The result is an inability to discern the heart of God and an asking that is askew.[6]

Most of us have a hard time accepting God's will when we don't understand why our prayers aren't being answered according to our expectations and hopes — especially if the results appear tragic. It's easy to become confused or angry about what God seems to be doing or not doing.

As a result, we may not know how to pray and God's will may seem hard to discern. At those times, we must pray in the best way we can. Clearly, our hearts and spirits must be submissive. A spirit of submission is at the heart of prayer. In this way, we often find God is changing us, helping us to submit to him. O. Hallesby describes this so clearly:

> When, therefore, the Spirit has taught us that God Himself decides when and how our prayers are to be answered, then we will experience rest and peace when we pray. We will begin to see that it is God's will not only to hear our prayer, but to give us the best and the richest answer which He, the almighty and omniscient God, can devise. He will send us the answer when it will benefit us and His cause the most. And He will send it to us in that way which will give us the best and most abiding results.[7]

Submission to God is the heart of prayer. We sometimes face situations that don't change. At such times, peace comes only as we rest in God's wisdom.

Faith-Seeded Prayer

Prayer as submission places faith in God in a *general* way, believing that he knows best and will give us what we need. However, there is another, related concept of prayer clearly presented in the Bible. Passage after passage in the New Testament asks us to exercise faith when we intercede, to pray for *particular* things, and to believe that the Lord will grant these requests. In these situations prayer is applied faith.

In Matthew 21, Jesus assures believers that faith will move mountains. He finishes his explanation with these words: "If you believe, you will receive whatever you ask for in prayer" (v. 22). When Jesus healed people during his ministry, he sometimes asked them about their faith. In Matthew 9, he asked two blind men, "Do you believe that I am able to do this?" (v. 28). James wrote, "Prayer offered in faith will make the sick person well" (James 5:15). Repeatedly we are told to ask in faith.

Jesus himself lived out this life of faith. Whether feeding the five thousand, healing the sick, or calming the storm, he prayed for particular things to happen, placing his faith in the Father.

Paul's epistles are powerful examples of his belief in prayer and the exercise of faith. In almost every letter, he asked his readers to pray for him specifically. In addition, Paul voiced prayers of faith for the people to whom he was writing. More than forty of Paul's prayers are recorded in the New Testament. In each of these passages, Paul both asked for prayer and prayed for others because he believed that God would hear and answer the prayer of faith.

Walking or Waiting

Prayer as submission, prayer as an act of faith — which is it? This thorny question isn't answered easily. It seems that prayer encompasses both of these concepts. Scripture instructs us to pray with particular needs in mind, believing in faith that God will answer. But God's call for us to bring specific requests to him in prayer does not negate his call for submission to his will.

We must live with the tension between prayer as submission and prayer as an expression of faith. We must both pray specific prayers in faith and submit to a sovereign God's answer. Faith isn't primarily a psychological experience or an emotional certitude; it's simply the conviction that God hears and answers prayer. Couples trust God when they bring their requests before him in faith and submit to his loving hand.

Part of the peace that comes in times of crisis is knowing that we have asked, that we have joined together as a couple and made the requests that are needed. Passivity breeds nothing but anxiety. Prayer — since it is an act of hope and trust — fosters peace in the midst of crisis.

Facing Our Faith

A few weeks after our son David died, we learned that Naomi had cancer. The news cut through us like a knife. The doctor told us chemotherapy should take care of it.

Once again, Naomi and I joined together in prayer. We prayed for her healing. Frankly, Naomi was afraid. She didn't trust the doctor's words about chemotherapy taking care of the cancer. With the recent experience of David's death, she was vividly aware of what God could allow into our lives.

These fears grew worse after the first course of chemotherapy. The report indicated that there had been no improvement. The doctors were concerned that the cancer was still there and decided that a second course was necessary. Naomi began to wonder if she, too, would die.

As Naomi and I prayed together one day, we had a time of silence. We waited on God, focused on listening. As we experienced his presence, I seemed to hear these simple words in my mind: "The Lord is a Rock. If you are standing on the Rock, all will be secure." I sensed that these words were for Naomi, and I shared them with her. Immediately, she experienced peace from God. In the weeks ahead, she found Scripture that affirmed these words, and sensed God's peace burrowing deeper and deeper into her heart. The first miracle was complete.

We continued to pray for Naomi to be healed — she had yet to begin her second course of treatments. One Sunday night, the senior pastor at the church where we ministered asked Naomi to come to the front of the church for prayer. Each of us extended our hands toward Naomi and prayed for her. The pastor asked Naomi to repeat these words: "I do not believe in the power of abnormal growths as much as I believe in the healing power of Christ within me."

Truthfully, Naomi didn't feel any change. But her peace continued and she rested in God's hands. Imagine our amazement when the next blood test, scheduled just before the second course of chemotherapy, revealed completely normal blood levels. God had healed Naomi — he'd miraculously, gloriously healed her! The second miracle was complete.

God had brought us full circle. From the difficult and heartbreaking death of our son, we learned submission to his will. From Naomi's glorious healing, we learned the prayer of faith.

A Place of Rest

I've known Dave and Arlene Wilson for several years because they are part of the church I pastor. They are a vibrant couple, close to God and to each other. They live out their lives in ministry to others, serving the congregation in many ways. I particularly admire Dave and Arlene because of their response to a major difficulty in their lives. You see, Arlene has multiple sclerosis, a disease of the central nervous system. It causes major disruptions in their lives.

The Wilsons have responded to God through this illness in a remarkable way. They have prayed for healing and asked others to pray also. Since God has chosen not to heal at this point, they have submitted to his will. They are at rest. However, this doesn't keep them from praying in faith for other needs. If Arlene has an infection, they pray in faith, asking God to heal. They know that God will take care of them. They understand the balance between submission and faith, and their priority is to stay connected to their Father.

God wants to bring peace into all our lives, regardless of our circumstances. We gain such peace in times of trouble when we come together and pray, affirming our trust in God and joining together in our pain. When we join with our spouse in prayer during times of crisis, we confess our dependence upon God and avoid the trap of arrogant self-reliance. We invite God to come crashing into the circumstances of our lives. The result? Peace. Unity. Rest.

Hard Times and Prayer Times

When an illness confines you to a bed. When a death thrusts you into grief. When a lost job risks the roof over your head. These are the times when God can feel a thousand miles away or as close as your heart — depending on the moment. These are also the times when praying together can leave an incredible legacy of faith and love. Its potential is worth discussing.

Where We're At (both answer)

1. When hard times have hit in the past, I've prayed:

a) Alone b) With you c) With someone else d) I haven't prayed at all

2. If you didn't pray together, what kept you from doing so?

3. What value do you think could come from praying together in a crisis?

Prompter: Comfort, discussion and ideas, confidence...

A Step Forward

Tell your partner one thing that would help you pray with him or her during a crisis.

Prompter: Persistence, a hug, a secret code word...

"Closet" Action

Select a problem (large or small) that you or someone you know is experiencing and pray about it together. Take note of how you feel when you hear your spouse talk to God about the problem. After praying, share what you felt.

CHAPTER EIGHT

Interceding for the Children in Our Lives

Sons are a heritage from the LORD, children a reward from him.
PSALMS 127:3

SOMETIMES I GO INTO MY CHILDREN'S BEDROOMS when they are asleep and pray for them. I remember looking down on my son Jon several years ago and being overcome with emotion. At eight years old he was so vulnerable, so small. And yet the energy in him! The potential! Standing there I felt the longing of a parent for Jon to mature into a man of God. I was moved to prayer as I realized that only the Lord could teach Jon all that he would need to know to walk the Christian life.

Most couples have children. When parents intercede together, they often center their attention on their children. Naomi and I have spent countless hours praying for our four kids. We have agreed together for God's intervention in their lives.

If you don't have children, you still *know* children. Perhaps you have nieces or nephews, or maybe you have a special relationship with the children of close friends. Perhaps you teach a Sunday school class that puts you in contact with little ones. Or maybe you're a foster parent.

Whatever your situation as a couple, you know children who need your intercession. Children seem to be at risk in new and insidious ways. All of us read the news enough to know of the breakup of the family, the secularization of our society, pedophilia and pornography, and other forces at work against children. The children we know need our prayers!

In chapter 3, we discussed the basics of interceding for others. In this chapter, we'll discuss some specific ways to intercede for the children we love.

How to Pray for Young Hearts

It's quite easy to slip into a pattern of praying for children that's all too general. "Lord, bless our children today" and "Lord, take care of Jon" are fine expressions of the heart, but we can go further. If you want to grow in your ability to intercede effectively for children, keep the following thoughts in mind.

Thanks for These Little Ones

One pattern evident in Paul's writing was that he invariably thanked God for the people for whom he was praying. First Thessalonians 1:2 is typical: "We always thank God for all of you, mentioning you in our prayers."

As we pray for our children, we can make a habit of thanking God for them. A spirit of thankfulness helps us maintain a good attitude. It reminds us that our children are a gift from God. Our family is God's creation! Parents generally feel thankful to God for their children, but it helps us to verbalize that thankfulness. It reminds us that they are precious, unique, and in need of our love and concern. Paul's example should encourage parents to find something positive to praise God for in their children, before they begin to intercede for them.

Help Them to Grow

If you've ever used a camera to take a picture, you know that one of the most basic skills needed is to frame the shot. The camera lens can only take in so much. We must decide what we will include in the picture before we snap the shutter.

In the same way, parents must be aware of the important areas in their children's lives that may need prayer, and decide where to concentrate. Luke 2:52 offers a pattern that may help you know what areas you can center on as you pray for your own children or for other kids God has placed on your heart. It says that Jesus "grew in wisdom and stature, and in favor with God and men." This statement suggests four growth areas in Jesus' development.

All of us read the news enough to know how much children need our prayers!

A spirit of thankfulness reminds us that our children are a gift from God.

As we release our children to God, we are released from fear.

Wisdom has to do with intellectual development, the growth of the mind. However, wisdom is not just knowledge; it is the godly application of that knowledge. Jesus' development in wisdom meant a growing knowledge of facts and the ability and sense to apply that knowledge.

Like many parents, Naomi and I pray that our children will do their best academically. We want them to have sharp minds and to develop those minds to the best of their abilities. But we also pray they will develop in their ability to apply knowledge appropriately and in a godly way. And we often pray that God will help our children discern between truth and error. One of our daughters is in high school. We pray that God will help her to be discerning about the things she is learning and to be aware when they do not mesh with God's Word. Sometimes, we pray specifically about a certain class or subject.

Luke goes on to say Jesus also grew in *stature*. Physical development and the health of our children is another area for which we should pray. When our children are sick, we pray for their healing. We pray for their physical protection during the day. We pray that God will keep them strong and healthy.

In today's world, the issue of physical safety is on many parents' hearts. Tales of random violence, child predators, and school problems seem to fill the newspapers. Naomi and I pray for our children's safety. As they walk out the door, we often remind them that God is going with them. It's a reminder we need as parents, too!

Jesus also grew in *favor with God*. Our children's spiritual development is perhaps the most important area for which to pray. After all, this will have eternal significance in their lives. Who they become in Christ in this life will provide a rich entrance into the next. It will also impact almost every other area of their lives in this world. To begin with, we pray that our children will enter a personal relationship with God. Once they've made that commitment, we can pray they will develop a hunger for spiritual things in their lives. In the moving prayer of David for his son Solomon, he prayed, "Give my son Solomon the wholehearted devotion to keep your commands"

(1 Chronicles 29:19). We need to echo this prayer. Naomi and I often pray that our children will grow in their love for God.

As parents become sensitive to the current needs of their children, they can pray specifically for their kids' spiritual development. Sometimes after children accept salvation, their spiritual needs tend to be ignored. We must continue to pray about specific areas of spirituality in our children's lives.

Finally, Jesus grew in *favor with men*. This pertains to social development. When we love kids, we want them to have good relationships with others. We want them to know how to get along with people and how to interact effectively. We pray for our children to be able to respect others and treat them well. We pray for our children's friends. Naomi and I sometimes pray for our children's future spouses. Children must learn to work, to live, to serve, and to play with others. If they do, good relationships will mark the rest of their lives. It's worth praying about!

Luke provided one pattern to follow in seeing specific areas for which we can intercede. However, it's good to remember that in praying for children, as in all prayer, we want to be led by the Holy Spirit, to hear his voice, and to pray in a way consistent with his will.

Show Us How to Lead

Before auto-focus cameras became so common, photographers had to twist a ring around the camera lens to bring a subject into focus. After framing a shot, they would make sure that the subject was clearly in focus before taking the picture. I've suggested general areas that we need to center on in our children's lives, but we can go further by focusing in on specifics. Like a photographer, framing the shot isn't enough — we must also focus in on the details. We can take each area in our children's lives and learn to pray specifically, according to the need.

Praying specifically for our children keeps us involved with them. We must *know* them in order to pray specifically for them. We must gain a sense of what their needs are and how to pray based on those needs. When we ask for God's will to come into their lives in a particular way, we are asking God to be involved in the individual needs of children.

How will we know how to pray for our children? Where do these specifics come from? Five activities provide information we can use to help us pray specifically for our own children and for any other child God places on our hearts.

Talk to your children. First, we must talk to our children! Direct conversation is the best way to ascertain their needs. You may remember your own preschooler coming to you and asking you to pray for their "owie," or some other need. Small children are sometimes spiritually sensitive and freely express such needs. But as children grow older, they often find it more difficult to express an exact need. Asking older children, "How can I pray for you?" may not help us figure out what they need.

That's where conversation comes in. We need to stay in contact with our children so that we know what is going on in their lives. Regular, meaningful conversation with our children can be difficult, especially in early adolescence. Studies show that in general, time spent in conversation between parents and children decreases during this time. Nevertheless, that is exactly what is needed.

This is one of the reasons why Naomi and I emphasize our evening meal as a family. It is a time of coming together, of making contact, and it gives us an ideal forum for conversation. What happened in school today? What was the best thing about today? How did that test go? How did you feel about not winning first place in the spelling bee? These are questions that can be asked. Wise parents take the opportunity to do a lot of listening.

Whether at dinner time, after school, or whenever, the idea is to recognize what is happening with our children and determine what their needs might be.

Recently, my daughter Jenny talked to me about the high school classes she would be registering for. As we talked, I could see that she wanted a specific schedule that she thought would meet her needs. It was important to her. After our conversation, I told her that her mother and I would be praying specifically that God would work out the schedule for her. Because she was open, I also took the opportunity to pray for her at that time. Without the conversation, I might not have known how to pray for this need.

It's also great to stay in touch with other children God brings into our lives. Teens in particular will sometimes relate better to an adult who is not their parent. We may be just the people God wants to listen to, support, and pray for those kids.

Observe your children. Having said that we should talk with our children, we must admit that our children don't or won't always tell us their needs. Though Paul could ask in 1 Thessalonians 5:25, "Brothers, pray for us," our children sometimes don't know what to ask for or how to ask.

That's why we need to be observing our kids. One of the things I watch for in my children is how they relate to people. How do they treat their friends, significant adults, teachers? When my son was ten years old, I became alert to a need in his life by watching him interact with another family with whom we were visiting. Several times during the evening, I realized he was being rude. Naturally, we talked to him directly and took steps to help him practically, but we also prayed that God would help him develop in this area.

It is all too easy in these busy days to tune out our children. Their behavior can relay important messages about what their needs are. We need to take the opportunities we have to see what is going on in their lives, and then act upon what we learn.

Listen to others. Listening to significant people in our children's lives can also help us know how to pray for our kids. Teachers, friends, youth pastors — all these people might have something significant to say. Certainly we shouldn't inappropriately intrude between our children and others. However, appropriate contact with people in our children's lives will alert us to specific needs.

The key here is simply to be in contact with the people who make a difference in our children's lives. We can create opportunities to have contact with their friends, for example. And we can establish ways to stay in contact with one or more of their teachers, such as attending parent-teacher conferences. We can talk directly with a youth pastor or Sunday school teacher who might have insight into our children.

Spend time with them. Implicit in all these ideas is the fundamental need to spend time with our children. I asked a woman how she knew what to pray for her children. She answered:

> We have seen many, many direct answers to prayer for our children. The key to knowing how to pray has been to spend time with them. Parents' time with their kids can be so minimal that they don't see how they habitually respond to others or to events in their lives. They're not making the minimal investment that's needed.

I don't quote this mother to heap guilt on other parents! Parenting can produce enough guilt without my adding to the burden. However, if you find that you lack the knowledge to pray effectively for your children, perhaps you should reconsider how much time you are spending with them.

"Ready-Made" Prayers

In his letters to various churches, Paul prays some forty prayers for his brothers and sisters in Christ. These prayers are a gold mine for those who wish to learn something about how to pray for the spiritual needs of others. They resound with a rich sense of Paul's hopes and godly desires for his fellow believers. Because of this, they are a wonderful resource in helping parents to pray for the spiritual development of their children.

Because Paul was a spiritual father to the believers he wrote to, there is a strong sense of parental concern in his writings. They are wonderful examples of how we can pray for our children. There are times when we may not know how to pray. When this happens, we can turn to Paul's "ready-made" prayers and know that what we're praying is God's will for our children.

As you use these prayers, do what is comfortable and natural for you. Sometimes you may simply want to personalize the prayer, using the written words almost verbatim. A short prayer in 2 Thessalonians 3:16 makes a good example. You might wish to pray, "Father, since you are the Lord of peace, please give Sarah peace at all times today and in every way."

You may wish to go further. After you use the "ready-made" prayer, you might want to make it specific to your children's specific needs. For example, "Father, I know that you are the Lord of peace. Please give Jenny peace at all times today. Let that peace extend to the school work she will be doing and the test she will take today. Help her to be calm and full of your peace as she takes the test."

You may want to simply use the prayer as a basis for praying in your own words — to paraphrase the prayer and apply it to your children. This might especially be appropriate with longer prayers. I have found that there is satisfaction in praying the exact words of Scripture, but I sometimes need to put the thoughts in my own words as well.

When we use a "ready-made" prayer, it helps to study the context in which the prayer appears. We can gain insights about how to pray for our children from the situations that the New Testament believers faced. Paying attention to the larger context also helps us not to misuse the Scriptures, but to pray in a way that is consistent with the original intent.

Let me show you how "ready-made" prayers from Paul's letters can help us pray for the spiritual needs of the children in our lives. The passages below are four of my favorite prayers. Why not experiment in praying for your children using these prayers? But don't stop there. Search the Scriptures yourself. You'll find many additional prayers. Use them as God leads.

Show Them Your Love

Ephesians 3:16–19

> *I pray that out of his glorious riches he may strengthen you with power through his Spirit in your inner being, so that Christ may dwell in your hearts through faith. And I pray that you, being rooted and established in love, may have power, together*

with all the saints, to grasp how wide and long and high and deep is the love of Christ, and to know this love that surpasses knowledge — that you may be filled to the measure of all the fullness of God.

This prayer is essentially a way of asking God to make the Ephesians completely aware of God's love for them. Paul asks that the Spirit help believers to let Christ be completely at home in their lives. As a result, they would have power to be aware of the magnitude of God's love for them, indeed that they would be filled to overflowing with the greatness of God's presence and love.

Does your son or daughter or niece or nephew need a fresh awareness of God's love for them? How about praying: "Father, I pray that the Spirit will give Tom the spiritual power to allow Christ to be completely at home in his life. Help him to grasp how wide and long and high and deep is the love of Christ for him. Fill him with a total awareness of your presence in his life. Thank you, Lord!"

Fill Them with Your Wisdom

Colossians 1:9–12

For this reason, since the day we heard about you, we have not stopped praying for you and asking God to fill you with the knowledge of his will through all spiritual wisdom and understanding. And we pray this in order that you may live a life worthy of the Lord and may please him in every way: bearing fruit in every good work, growing in the knowledge of God, being strengthened with all power according to his glorious might so that you may have great endurance and patience, and joyfully giving thanks to the Father, who has qualified you to share in the inheritance of the saints in the kingdom of light.

What we see here are five steps that take place over time to produce Christian growth. Step one: Gain an ongoing knowledge of what the Bible says ("filled with a knowledge of His will"). Step two: Correctly respond to God's Word with a personal application to my life ("in all spiritual wisdom and understanding"). Step three: Act upon this application to actually please God in my behavior ("live a life worthy of the Lord, to please him"). Step four: The natural order of knowing, responding, and acting upon God's Word is to bear fruit ("bearing fruit in every good work"). Step five: Grow in character and continue on in the process ("increasing in the knowledge of God"). All of this is a lifelong process, a process that we want to see our children actively involved in throughout their lives.

How can we use this in prayer? "Father, I'm praying today for Dennis. Fill him with your will. Give him a hunger for your Word. As he reads the Bible, help him to know what you are saying. Give him spiritual wisdom and understanding so that he can apply the Scripture to himself. I'm especially praying today that you would help him to apply your Word to his anger. Help him to see your plan for himself in that area. Then Lord, help him to live out what you are telling him; help him to please you today. Thank you, Lord, that as he finds and applies your will for his life, fruit will result and he will be strengthened and full of joy and thanksgiving, according to your Word. Amen."

Strengthen Their Hearts

1 Thessalonians 3:12–13

> *May the Lord make your love increase and overflow for each other and for everyone else, just as ours does for you. May he strengthen your hearts so that you will be blameless and holy in*

the presence of our God and Father when our Lord Jesus comes with all his holy ones.

Two simple requests are listed here: for love to increase and for hearts to be strengthened. If these two things were present, the Thessalonians would overflow in their love for each other and be able to live a holy life and meet the Lord confidently when he returns.

"Lord, I'm praying today that you will increase Bob's love for you and for others. I pray that love will begin to overflow first here in the home, then in his many other relationships. Help him to treat others with your love. And, Father, please strengthen his heart so that he can be the man you want him to be, holy and blameless before you. Thank you, Lord."

Be Glorified in Their Lives

2 Thessalonians 1:11–12

With this in mind, we constantly pray for you, that our God may count you worthy of his calling, and that by his power he may fulfill every good purpose of yours and every act prompted by your faith. We pray this so that the name of our Lord Jesus may be glorified in you, and you in him, according to the grace of our God and the Lord Jesus Christ.

I love this passage! It is literally asking God to give power to the Thessalonians to fulfill every act and every purpose which is prompted by their faith. The name of Jesus would be glorified as his will was accomplished through their lives.

"Father, today I'm praying that you will fulfill every good purpose that you have for Tina's life as she moves in faith. Help her to trust you, to hear from you, and to resolve to do things your way for this day. Father, give her success in each act that is prompted by her trust in you. May the name of Jesus be lifted up and glorified in her as she moves ahead in you. Thank you, Lord!"

Rebel with a Prayer

Problems and conflicts are absolutely normal in our kids' lives. Not wanting to do chores, not maintaining a clean room, putting off homework, watching too much TV, sometimes resisting going to church, teasing brothers and sisters — these are all an ordinary part of growing up. Issues of character-building and spiritual growth will always exist in our families. These normal kid problems are tremors compared to the jolting earthquake of active and deep-rooted rebellion. Some parents will be faced with incredible challenges if their children negotiate a more dangerous journey. This is a time when, more than ever, parents need to unite in prayer — not only for the sake of their rebel, but also for the sake of their marriage.

These are the parents who must deal with children who stay out past curfew, run away from home, skip school, fail classes, take or sell drugs, drink alcoholic beverages, shoplift, or run with a bad crowd. These problems are very serious and definitely create a high degree of stress — and an enormous need for prayer!

Obviously, this book cannot begin to answer the questions for parents who walk this difficult path. For that reason I recommend Buddy Scott's book *Relief for Hurting Parents*. It gives concrete suggestions for parents who need to help fight for the lives of their children.

So how do we pray for kids who are on the edge? First of all we must intercede for them. We may need to engage in spiritual warfare on their behalf — kids today face incredible foes, and most of them they aren't even aware of... We also need to ask God for daily wisdom and help in our parenting skills. Facing these new challenges is a lot like pioneering unnavigated territory — God's wisdom is our compass, his Word is our map.

He's Your Child, God

Dennis began to rebel as a teen. Choosing the wrong friends rapidly progressed to his becoming sexually active. More than one of his girlfriends became pregnant. It was a nightmare for his parents, Tim and Rachel. Prayer became their lifeline.

After a while, their prayers took an abrupt turn. Instead of focusing their petitions on help and rescue for Dennis, they sensed God leading them in a new direction.

"As we prayed, we were impressed to allow God to be God and to stay out of it," Rachel explained. "We prayed and decided we would not rescue Dennis if his choices got him into trouble. In fact, we prayed specifically that God would do whatever it took to bring him around." Tim and Rachel took a brave step by releasing their son into God's hands. This is one of the most difficult acts of faith a parent can undertake.

We, as parents, are responsible for our own choices and must act responsibly in dealing with our children. However, we don't have the power to reach into our children's hearts and change them. A friend helped Rachel by telling her, "Parents must refuse to take the blame for their children's choices — and refuse to take the credit when things turn around!" When Tim and Rachel released Dennis to God, they reminded themselves that they were only stewards of their son's life — Dennis belonged to God! Parents can teach and love and pray, but their children must ultimately make a decision to respond. This is between each child and God.

As we release our children to God, we are released from fear. "Fear would rip us apart," Rachel said. "Over and over again, I would pray Scripture into our lives about God's ability to overcome fear." In releasing their son, they placed him safely into God's hands where he belonged. As a result, they were able to live their lives without overwhelming and disabling fear.

Another difficult situation where parents must release their children to God happens when couples share child custody after a divorce. These parents don't have the consistent daily input into their children's lives that they would like. I'm personally aware of several single parents whose hearts ache when their children are away. Releasing your children to God is the key. It lets you rest in the knowledge that they are in God's care and that you trust him with their well-being.

Don't Give Up

Parents need to embrace another important guideline relating to praying for their children: Don't give up. Tim and Rachel spent a good deal of time praying for Dennis, but seldom saw any change. Rachel told me, "Usually when we prayed he got worse! I got so I could hardly pray for him." Fortunately, Tim and Rachel had good friends who supported them and helped them to pray.

One of the gospel's most encouraging parables about prayer begins with this intriguing sentence: "Then Jesus told his disciples a parable to show them that they should always pray and not give up" (Luke 18:1). The parable is of the "how much more" variety. That is, if an unrighteous judge will meet the need of a widow because of her constantly asking, *How much more?*, will God be ready to meet the needs of his children? The point is this: Always pray; don't give up.

Tim and Rachel's son had to go through many difficulties before he began making better choices. Through it all, his parents prayed. Diagnosed with the HIV virus, Dennis made his way to a local church. He responded by asking for prayer after the service. In an amazing demonstration of how God works, the stranger who prayed for Dennis had lost a son to AIDS. Dennis responded to God as this man prayed.

Never underestimate God's power in a person's life or his ability to sovereignly arrange circumstances for the benefit of his children. Keep praying, parents, and don't give up!

Supernatural Parenting

No matter how many diapers are changed, basketball games attended, or family rules enforced, a parent knows they're working from the outside in. What will motivate, what will hurt, what will encourage, what will trigger rebellion — these are the unknowns every parent faces. These are the reasons mom and dad need to take their kids before the One "who looks on the heart."

Where We're At (both answer)

1. Have you ever prayed with your spouse for your children? How often?

a. If no or infrequently, tell your spouse one or more reasons why you haven't.

Prompter: Not in the habit, differences in parenting...

b. If yes, tell your spouse the benefit you have seen from it.

Prompter: Aware of kids' needs, not on your own...

A Step Forward

Is there something you can do that would encourage, or continue to encourage, your spouse to pray for the kids together?

"Closet" Action

Take some time to discuss your children as individuals — problems, strengths, attitudes.... Then pray for each one, thanking God for the positives, as well as asking him to fix the negatives.

CHAPTER NINE

Resisting the Evil One

*Put on the full armor of God so that you can
take stand against the devil's schemes.*

EPHESIANS 6:12

SOMETHING HAPPENED WHILE I WAS WRITING this book that illustrates our need to resist the evil one — Satan. I'm naturally an optimistic, "up" person. However, over a period of two or three months I began to leave church feeling depressed.

As senior pastor, I lead weekly services and preach a sermon. After church, I started having negative thoughts: *The congregation didn't seem to get anything from the message; I really wasn't very effective; this isn't going too well.* After a few minutes of thinking like this, I'd feel pretty discouraged. I began to dread services and the feelings of defeat that came afterward.

This situation called for "resisting prayer," or what is sometimes termed "spiritual warfare." One chapter cannot begin to explain every aspect of this large topic, but we can discuss some basic concepts that will help us to resist the evil one as we pray together.

What Is "Resisting Prayer"?

In Matthew 6:13 Jesus teaches us to pray to be delivered from the enemy's influence in our lives.

This isn't the only place where we're encouraged to resist the devil. "Put on the full armor of God," wrote Paul, "so that you can take your stand against the devil's schemes" (Ephesians 6:11). Peter told believers that "the devil prowls around like a roaring lion looking for someone to devour. Resist him" (1 Peter 5:8–9).

Thomas B. White further clarifies the spiritual battle we face when he describes the difference between direct and indirect spiritual warfare:

> To say that a Christian struggles with *direct* spiritual warfare is to describe some form of hand-to-hand combat, a tangible interference of intelligent evil beings with a child of God. This direct warfare is precisely what Paul describes so vividly in Ephesians 6 with the image of the soldier warding off "flaming arrows." Such warfare may involve enticement toward a specific sin, such as explosive anger or indulgence in pornography. Or it might manifest itself as doubt introduced into the mind of a believer who is weak in faith, or despondency undermining the fragile emotions of one who is wrestling with low self-esteem. In such cases, a real spirit is tangibly present and is committed to carrying out an assignment against a child of God. "Oppression" is the alien pressure that makes the normal challenges of life more difficult than they should be.
>
> To say, on the other hand, that a Christian faces *indirect* spiritual warfare is to acknowledge that the devil and his

forces exert a broad influence over the affairs of life, that indeed "the whole world is under the control of the evil one" (1 John 5:19).[1]

Resisting prayer, simply put, is any prayer that opposes the direct or indirect influence of the evil one.

These Bible passages and concepts don't need to scare Christian couples. God wants us to be alert so that we can resist rather than be frightened into inaction. It's easier to resist when we know our position relative to that of Satan.

Where We Stand

First, we should know the devil is a defeated enemy. According to Scripture, "The reason the Son of God appeared was to destroy the devil's work" (1 John 3:8). In the broadest sense of the word, Satan's diabolic plan is blocked because of Christ's work on the cross. Paul told the Colossian believers, "Having disarmed the powers and authorities, he made a public spectacle of them, triumphing over them by the cross" (Colossians 2:15). These and other Scriptures proclaim: Satan is ultimately defeated.

Next we should know that while Satan has no *authority* to harm us, he will attempt to undermine our relationship with Christ. Satan's ultimate defeat is assured, but he continues doing all he can to hinder God's people until the Lord's return.

That's why we're told to take a stand against "the devil's schemes" (Ephesians 6:11) and why Paul describes a "struggle" in which believers are engaged with the "powers of this dark world" (6:12). If we don't know how to use our position in Christ, we may face difficulties.

While it's essential to realize that "the one who is in you is greater than the one who is in the world" (1 John 4:4), we must also know that God wants us to exercise faith in the practical outworking of this position. That's why we are told to "take up the shield of faith, with which you can extinguish all the flaming arrows of the evil one" (Ephesians 6:16).

Making a Stand

The phrase "resisting prayer" describes the position we take when we challenge Satan's power through our prayers. This warfare-style of prayer doesn't always fit into daily prayer-time, nor is it confined to a certain prayer lap. Naomi and I sometimes pray, "God help us now to be alert to the schemes of the enemy. Help us to discern any way in which we should pray." We invite God's help, then wait for a moment. Sometimes we're led to pray in a specific way. Most often, we realize that when we intercede for someone, we also need to pray against Satan's stronghold in their life — or in other words, "resisting evil." We frequently use this strategy when we pray about things that affect our family or church. Since both these institutions are God's creations, Satan goes out of his way to try and bring them down.

How do we "resist Satan" while praying together? Although we're still learning about this element of prayer, let me share a strategy that's been part of our prayer life for many years. How often we utilize this type of prayer depends on how we're led to pray by the Holy Spirit. But when necessary, we don't hesitate to move in this direction during prayer.

Binding the Enemy

Jesus gives a key principle for resisting the devil in Matthew 12:25–29. He says in part, "How can anyone enter a strong man's house and carry off his possessions unless he first ties up the strong man?" In Jesus' analogy, the "strong man" is clearly Satan. When believers need to reclaim something from the devil, Jesus explains, they must first "bind him." When a couple discerns that Satan is trying to hinder their lives or the life of someone in their family or church, they must call upon God's authority to *bind the strongman* — Satan — who's trying to work his will to devour and destroy.

"Binding the enemy" means asking God to restrain Satan's work in the lives of people for whom we're praying. *We* don't bind the enemy; *God* does. Jesus established such a pattern in his treatment of Satan. In Luke 9:42 (and on other occasions), Jesus rebuked an unclean spirit. During Christ's temptation, he turned back Satan's schemes with Scripture and then simply told Satan, "Away from me" (Matthew 4:10). He had authority to rebuke the work of the enemy. Satan is subject to God and cannot escape his ultimate will. Asking God to rebuke Satan means asking him to restrict Satan's influence, his "scheme," in a person's life.

Naomi and I pray something like this: "Father, we believe that the enemy is tempting Jon in this area. We ask you to overcome Satan now, in Jesus' name. We agree with your Word that the blood of Jesus has paid the price for Jon and that Satan is defeated in his life. Bind the enemy from tempting Jon in Jesus' name."

It caught me by surprise when I experienced the defeat I described at the beginning of this chapter. At first, I wasn't sure how to respond. Then one day, while driving alone and feeling lousy, something extraordinary happened. Just as I was thinking, *The services are not effective,* a different idea flew into my mind. It seemed as if God was speaking to me. God's message was simple but effective: "These thoughts are not from me but from the enemy." I simply hadn't considered the fact that I was being harassed by the enemy.

My response? I began to pray, asking God for discernment. As I prayed, it became clear that I had just experienced one of the "devil's schemes." It was a "flaming dart." I continued to pray with fresh energy: "Father, I pray right now that you'll bind any spirit of discouragement or any other satanic force trying to hinder my effectiveness as a pastor." Something heavy was lifted off me, and I stopped experiencing those discouraging thoughts after church services.

God is involved in our lives, and we can experience the presence of the Holy Spirit and his direction daily. A spiritual world exists outside our senses. That day in my car, God gave me discernment about a scheme of the enemy and then answered my prayer to squelch that scheme.

Pulling Down Strongholds

There's a second part to the strategy for resisting the enemy: discerning and destroying satanic strongholds. In Ephesians 4:27 Paul told believers, "Do not give the devil a foothold." A "foothold" might be defined as any deliberate sin by a believer which Satan can use for greater evil. For example, if someone chooses to stay bitter, Satan is given a foothold through which he can cause great difficulty in that person's relationships. Over time, a foothold can develop into a "stronghold."

This concept is discussed in 2 Corinthians 10:4: "The weapons we fight with are not the weapons of the world. On the contrary, they have divine power to demolish strongholds." A stronghold in this verse might be defined as a satanically inspired resistance to God's will. Thomas B. White defines a stronghold as "an entrenched pattern of thought, an ideology, value, or behavior that is contrary to the Word and will of God."[2]

Suppose a son or daughter is caught up in drug abuse or some other form of rebellion. Mental and spiritual barriers to God's truth are erected in his to her life. It may seem that the Bible and the things of God can't penetrate. They have given the devil a foothold, and now a stronghold has developed.

As we pray together with our spouse, the Holy Spirit can show us how to discern strongholds. A stronghold might be indicated if the Holy Spirit alerts you to any "footholds" in a person's life. These are areas where a person seems to have little or no control. Maybe you heard someone say, "I'm stuck in this sin," or "I'll never change," or "I'm worthless." Satan may have established a beachhead, a resistance to God's will that hampers that believer.

God wants us to be alert so that we can resist rather than being frightened into inaction.

Prayer is used to knock down thoughts that counter the will of God.

How can we pray if such a stronghold is detected? Second Corinthians 10:4 suggests that the weapons God gives us have "divine power" to "demolish strongholds." Again, *we* can't demolish strongholds; *God* can. The Greek word for "demolish" can be translated "pull down." How do we pull down a stronghold? Any soldier must have weapons with which to fight. These weapons are detailed in Ephesians 6 as truth, righteousness, evangelism, faith, salvation, the Word of God, and prayer. Prayer is used to pull down thoughts that counter the will of God.

Years ago, Naomi and I discerned that Satan was hindering a friend (I'll call him "Eric"). We began to sense that something in Eric prevented him from responding to his wife. We asked God to guide us to pray in a way that would help him.

After some time, we sensed that a stronghold of pride kept Eric from getting close to his wife. We prayed like this: "Father, we ask you to expose the enemy's schemes in Eric's life. Pull down this stronghold of pride and replace it with obedience to your Word. Release Eric from pride so that he can love his wife. Help him to repent where he has disobeyed you in this area. Thank you, Lord." We then began to pray that God's Word would penetrate Eric's life so that he could be responsive to what God wanted him to do.

You might be saying, "Hold it, doesn't the person affected have anything to say?" Of course. Praying that God will pull down Satan's stronghold doesn't take away individual responsibility. They still must hear and respond to the Word of God. However, when a stronghold is in place, a person's ability to hear from God seems affected. "Arguments" and "pretensions" set themselves up "against the knowledge of God" (2 Corinthians 10:5) in such a way that these people continue to be deceived. For complete victory over a stronghold, the bound person must choose to close the door to the devil's lies.

Praying for God's Protection

Finally, this "resisting prayer" strategy includes praying for God's protection. There's no special formula — we simply call upon the Lord for protection and help, and he will deliver us. "'Because he loves me,' says the LORD, 'I will rescue him; He will call upon me, and I will answer him.... I will deliver him'" (Psalms 91:14–15).

A central verse to consider here is 2 Thessalonians 3:3: "But the Lord is faithful, and he will strengthen and protect you from the evil one." God's protection is bound up in the sacrifice of Jesus' blood for our sins. Colossians 1:13–14 says, "For he has rescued us from the dominion of darkness and brought us into the kingdom of the Son he loves, in whom we have redemption, the forgiveness of sins." We have been transferred from Satan's kingdom to the "kingdom of the Son."

The agent of that transfer was the blood of Jesus. "How much more, then, will the blood of Christ…cleanse our consciences from acts that lead to death" (Hebrews 9:14). Sin should have led to death, should have placed us under Satan's power, but Jesus took away that authority by dying in our place. His blood is the agent which takes away Satan's authority in our lives. Every believer is free from darkness, free from the enemy's demands. The blood of Christ destroyed the works of the devil.

When Naomi and I pray for God's protection, we might pray this way:

> Father, since your Word declares that you will protect your children from the evil one, we pray that you will shield_____from the power and influence of the enemy. Thank you that your blood has delivered us from Satan's kingdom and taken away his authority. We place_____under the authority of your blood right now. Be a shield of light against the enemy's schemes. Send your angels to guard_____from danger and to block the devil's strategy. Since you have a will for_____, let your will be done.

"Resisting prayer" won't always be a part of your regular prayer time. After all, not every problem has a satanic origin. We all have our own sin nature to deal with as well. However, Jesus' words "deliver us from the evil one" and many other Scriptures say something about praying against the devil's schemes. Even those we pray for who have *primarily* psychological or social problems may need resisting prayer to bind the hand of the enemy in those areas.

The Holy Spirit must give us discernment about when and how to pray in this way. He'll help us distinguish between spiritual problems and those that are physical, psychological, or social. We're told that the Holy Spirit "searches all things" and that through the Spirit, God reveals truth to believers (1 Corinthians 2:10).

Secondly, the Bible itself helps believers discern satanic influence in a person's life. The Scriptures say, "For the word of God is living and active.... It judges the thoughts and attitudes of the heart. Nothing in all creation is hidden from God's sight" (Hebrews 4:12–13). To the degree that the Holy Spirit and the Word of God help us discern satanic involvement, "resisting prayer" is our logical and appropriate response.

If you can't agree with each other about this aspect of prayer, don't despair. You can agree to disagree. It's natural for a couple to have different opinions about this issue. If you agree on the substance of this chapter, try adding "resisting prayer" to your prayer times together when the Holy Spirit leads you to do so.

Tackling the Front Line

Whether soldiers faced Normandy's beaches, Vietnam's jungles, the Middle East's deserts or Bosnia's mined fields, none of them wanted to be on the front line. It's dangerous. It's scary. Even though we know the outcome of the invisible battle around us, God's spiritual front line can be just a forbidding. As a result it's easy to avoid them, even though we often feel their impact. It is this impact, that makes discussing them important.

Where We're At (both answer)

1. How does this chapter make you feel? What past experiences or thoughts support your reaction to it?

Prompter: Fear of unknown, empowerment, hocus-pocus...

2. Do you think we're sometimes on a spiritual front line and need to utilize the power of "resisting prayer"? Why?

Prompter: See needs in others, what Bible says...

A Step Forward

1. If spiritual warfare is real to you, do you think facing it with a partner would be helpful? If so, tell your spouse why.

2. If spiritual warfare or your role in it isn't real to you, read together some of the Bible passages mentioned in this chapter and discuss them honestly together.

"Closet" Action

If spiritual warfare is a hard issue for one or both of you, talk to God about it. Tell him the truth, even if you think it's boo-in-the-dark stuff. But then ask him to *show* you truth. If spiritual warfare is a settled issue between you and God, discuss a situation in your lives that may be affected by it. Then do some "resisting" prayer.

CHAPTER TEN

Hearing God's Voice

...be still, and know that I am God.

PSALMS 46:10

WHEN I WAS IN SEMINARY, I studied Christian counseling. In one of my first classes, we talked about the various skills needed to effectively enter another person's world. One of the most basic skills was listening. I'd never thought of listening as a skill before: something to learn, an ability in which I could grow.

In the same way, listening to God is a spiritual skill in which any of us can grow. Perhaps you didn't realize that God can speak to you. Or maybe you question whether you're able to hear him. Think again. Listening prayer is not for the privileged few or the mega-spiritual. It is for every believer.

In the Presence of the One You Love

Hearing God's voice boils down to one simple function: listening. We learn to be silent, to feel his presence, to listen to his voice, and to respond. When listening to God becomes part of a couple's prayer time, it leads to a deeper relationship with God, and contributes a vital component to any couple's prayer adventure.

To listen in prayer is literally to meet with God. It's the difference between sending a letter to someone, receiving no immediate response, and having an actual meeting with someone to exchange ideas and thoughts, to both talk and listen. Listening when we pray creates an encounter, an event at which we are present with God. In such an environment, we are open and willing to hear from our Lord.

Of all the benefits that come from praying together, perhaps the greatest benefit is a growing awareness of God's presence. When couples make a habit of coming to God in prayer, they are practicing the presence of God. A deepening relationship with God is the result.

Madame Jeanne Guyon, a seventeenth-century believer who spent almost twenty-five years in prison for her religious beliefs, wrote eloquently of listening for God's presence:

> Once your heart has been turned inwardly to the Lord, you will have an impression of his presence. You will be able to notice his presence more acutely because your outer senses have now become very calm and quiet. The Lord's chief desire is to reveal himself to you. He touches you, and his touch is so delightful that, more than ever, you are drawn inwardly to him.[1]

She's right: the Lord wants to reveal himself to us. To some degree, we seem to have lost the sense of wonder in God's presence. Certainly the psalmists treasured God's presence as their chief reward. David cried out to God in the Sixty-third Psalm with an intense desire for the Lord: "O God, you are my God, earnestly I see you; my soul thirsts for you, my body longs for you, in a dry and weary land where there is no water" (63:1). What is David after? God's presence — a spiritual relationship that is likened to a physical need.

Couples must remember that they spend time with God not only to get something done but also to develop a relationship with their Father. Anselm, an eleventh-century Christian and an enlightened thinker who later became Archbishop of Canterbury, displayed a humorous and insightful approach to God in prayer. He wrote the following as a call to meditation:

Come now, little man, turn aside for a while from your daily employment, escape for a moment from the tumult of your thoughts. Put aside your weighty cares, let your burdensome distractions wait, free yourself awhile for God and rest awhile in him. Enter the inner chamber of your soul, shut out everything except God and that which can help you in seeking him, and when you have shut the door, seek him. Now, my whole heart, say to God, "I seek your face, Lord, it is your face I seek."[2]

"When you have shut the door, seek him." As we pray together with our spouse, more than anything, we seek God and his presence. We are "shutting out everything except God." Like the psalmists, we are rewarded with a growing sense of God's presence and a deepening relationship with him. Listening prayer can be a major part of becoming aware of God's presence.

Listening: The Interchange of Love

Philip Yancey wrote:

The art of prayer is one we should have mastered by now, but I have my doubts. We are constantly tempted to turn prayer into another form of work, which may explain why prayers in evangelical churches major on intercession. We bring God our wish lists and rarely get around to listening.[3]

Yancey is right: most of us rarely get around to listening. When we pray consistently without the element of listening, prayer can become sterile and lifeless. As we parade out our needs to God over and over, there is no *relationship,* no give and take. And that, after all, is what we want most of all in prayer, an interchange of love. A. W. Tozer said it this way:

He thinks, wills, enjoys, feels, loves, desires and suffers as any other person may. In making Himself known to us He stays by the familiar pattern of personality. He communicates with us through the avenues of our minds, our wills and our emotions. The continuous and unembarrassed interchange of love and thought between God and the soul of the redeemed man is the throbbing heart of New Testament religion.[4]

Listening prayer recognizes that prayer is an exchange, that prayer can be a conversation. It recognizes that God can speak to us in what Richard Foster calls the "divine whisper."[5] Those who grew up in the church have heard the phrase, "the still, small voice." God speaks to us as couples in such a voice.

Most of us like to stick to the clearly marked highways of prayer: But the way to listening prayer is less distinct, more like a path or trail. We like to talk — we know *how* to talk with God, but it's harder to listen. We strain and wonder, *Have we heard? Is this God?*

Saints throughout the ages have sought God in this way and found the rich treasure of his presence. Madame Jeanne Guyon said, "Rest. Rest. Rest in God's love. The only work you are required now to do is to give your most intense attention to His still, small voice within."[6] Leslie Weatherhead began his daily prayer this way: "As I bow in the quiet room I have made in my heart, O Lord, let the hush of thy presence fall upon me."[7]

The goal of listening prayer is to be present with God and, if he wishes to speak, to hear his voice. Listening prayer means primarily to be in the "hush of his presence," and thus open to hearing his voice. Sometimes that means we sense God saying something to us, even something as simple as, "I love you." At other times, we end our time of prayer without any specific word from God, but with an unswerving sense that we have been with him. Just the practice of spending time with our spiritual ears open is important. As we do this, we will experience a growing awareness of what God may wish to communicate to us by his Spirit.

We want to experience such an awareness of God so we can be sensitive to his thoughts, his ideas, his direction, and his love. One Scripture that seems to invite such union is Jesus' prayer in John 15:4: "Remain in me, and I will remain in you." Synonyms for "remain" include "indwell," "abide with," and "live in" Christ. This verse is talking about a living, growing union with Jesus. That union demands a listening ear.

As couples, we need to pray in a way that allows for God's involvement. Conversational prayer will naturally have silent periods. Many times, silence can be awkward in a conversation. However, silence in the context of prayer is a way of observing one of the components of any conversation — listening.

Don't be afraid of silent periods. God can speak in silence. Sometimes you'll be led to ask God a question such as this: "What do you want in this situation?" Questions like this one create natural times to pause and listen, and to anticipate God to speak. Pray knowing that the God who loves you will answer you. Pray with a heart that is open and expectant, seeking the voice of God at that moment and in the moments to come.

Hearing Our Master's Voice

Larry and Ruth went to their dentist for their regular checkup. Quite innocently, they learned that a member of their church was in debt to this dentist and hadn't been able to make the debt good. Later, they began to pray for this man, asking God to provide what was needed financially.

As they paused in prayer one day, Larry heard this from God: "You pay the man's dentist bill." No Bible verse, no brilliant shaft of sunlight from the sky. Just the words: "You pay the bill." Larry shared what he thought he was hearing with Ruth and she swallowed hard. It was a sizable amount and would be a stretch for them. Nonetheless, they decided to do what they believed God had told them to do.

Months later, this act of service had touched the dentist, the man in debt, and several others. Though not a Christian, the dentist gained new respect for this church and the gospel message. Paying the bill encouraged the dentist, and his good report made its way to several others over the months that followed. All this because Larry and Ruth had listened to and obeyed God's voice.

Listen to the Word. Does God speak? My reading of the New Testament convinces me that God speaks to us in two primary ways. His most basic communication to us comes through his written Word, the Bible. One vital way to listen to God is to prayerfully consider what he has already revealed in his Word and how to apply that to our lives. As we are quiet before God, he may bring a Scripture to mind that we know is intended for us. Couples who quiet their hearts and read the Bible as part of their prayer time together soon find that God is speaking to them through his Word.

Heed that still small voice. Second, God can speak to us through the Holy Spirit. Paul said in Romans, "You, however, are controlled not by the sinful nature but by the Spirit, if the Spirit of God lives in you. And if anyone does not have the Spirit of Christ, he does not belong to Christ" (8:9). The Spirit of God lives in every Christian. Most of us can point to times when the Spirit has spoken to us on some level. Perhaps we simply felt the Spirit bringing conviction into our lives, or maybe in prayer we sensed that we should do something specific. That is the Spirit's work in our lives.

The early history of the church is full of examples of the Spirit of God speaking. Acts 13:1–3 depicts the account of the Spirit's direction for a missionary journey. "While they were worshiping the Lord and fasting, the *Holy Spirit said*" (13:2; italics added). God spoke! His children listened. In Acts 15 the Jerusalem Council wrote to the Gentile believers: "It *seemed good to the Holy Spirit* and to us" (15:28; italics added). The implication is that the Holy Spirit gave direction to the council. God spoke! His children listened. In Acts 18:9 the Spirit of Christ spoke to Paul in a vision that encouraged him in his work. God spoke! His child listened.

> *Most of us like to stick to the clearly marked highways of prayer: the way to listening prayer is less distinct, more like a path or trail.*
>
> *The goal of listening prayer is to be present with God and, if he wishes to speak, to hear his voice.*
>
> *Don't be afraid of silent periods. God can speak in silence.*

In one conversation, Paul said simply: "But God has revealed it to us by his Spirit" (1 Corinthians 2:10). Paul goes on to say that believers have received the Spirit "that we may understand what God has freely given us" (2:12). Part of the Spirit's function is to reveal God's plan to us. We have a living, personal relationship with God, and that includes two-way communication because the Holy Spirit lives in us. The promptings of the Holy Spirit have not been lost to our generation.

If God speaks through His Spirit, how does it happen? That is the more difficult question. Sometimes believers make statements like "God told me" or "God said to me." I am more comfortable with phrases such as "What I seem to be hearing" or "God seems to be saying to me." Tom White warns against being presumptuous about what we hear:

> Of course, if it is taken to an extreme this matter of following promptings and impressions can lead to a reckless "God told me" syndrome or to a "Thus saith the Lord" judgment spoken about a person or situation. Such impressions can originate from human intention. Sad to say, these faulty leadings have served to discredit the valid leadings that *are* from God and *do* bear fruit.[8]

Having said that the promptings of the Holy Spirit can be misread or misrepresented, we must not push aside the genuine touch of the Holy Spirit upon the lives of countless believers. God wants to speak to us through his Spirit.

Listening Together

There are four methods God often uses to help Naomi and me, and other Christians, hear his voice. These are not offered as the norm for anyone else, but as concrete examples for those who are asking the question: How might God speak?

A Reflection

In a recent prayer seminar a woman explained that she sometimes heard God when he brought to her memory a certain verse from the Bible. A Bible reference or the words themselves came to mind, and she sensed that this was God speaking to her. Many of us can recall a similar experience, a time when the Holy Spirit applied a specific Bible verse to our heart. Certainly, that is God speaking to us.

A Song

Sometimes when we are in God's presence, we experience an emotion which we sense is from God. Perhaps I have been still before the Lord for a few moments. The Spirit inside seems to be "stirring" me. When I try to put that emotion into words, it becomes apparent that this is what God is wanting to say to me. A. W. Tozer described the experience this way:

> Every one of us has had experiences which we have not been able to explain: a sudden sense of loneliness, or a feeling of wonder or awe in the face of the universal vastness. Or we have had a fleeting visitation of light like an illumination from some other sun, giving us in a quick flash an assurance that we are from another world, that our origins are divine, that such experiences may arise from the Presence of God.[9]

At times like that, we may feel awe as we realize that God is speaking to us.

A Whisper

Sometimes Naomi or I actually hear inside our mind a phrase or idea that we sense is from God. Often this happens when we are being quiet before the Lord, or when we have asked him a question. Such times are a part of our relationship with God. Recently, as we sat quietly with the Lord, I heard this phrase: "If you give all, I will supply all." God's voice through the Spirit is not audible to me at these times. But I have the definite impression that God is speaking without words, that he is communicating with me.

A Vision

At other times when in God's presence, I see a picture in my mind's eye that is from God. As I remain tuned to God and ask him what the picture is about, I seem to hear his explanation.

At still other times, God takes a real picture, something in my physical world, and uses that to talk to me. This would be similar to his conversation with Abraham in Genesis 15. He took Abraham outside to look at the stars and then spoke to him using that picture: "Look up at the heavens and count the stars.... So shall your offspring be" (Genesis 15:5).

I expect there are other ways to listen to God in prayer. Since God has made each one of us unique, we may each have our own sense of how God speaks to us. These four avenues are simply some of what is meant when a Christian says, "God spoke to me."

Recognizing Our Master's Voice

How do we know when something is from God? That's difficult to explain. The whole issue of *knowing* spiritual things is a complex. We know spiritual things because the Spirit of God reveals them to us.

Thus, Paul could say that "God has revealed it to us by his Spirit" (1 Corinthians 2:10).

So now the question becomes, How do we know the Spirit has spoken? This places us in the realm of faith. "Now faith is being sure of what we hope for and certain of what we do not see" (Hebrews 11:1). By faith, the heroes of Hebrews 11 believed that they had heard from God and chose to act upon what they heard. For me, this sense of "knowing" is the quiet quickening that happens in my mind and heart when I sense, "Yes, this is it. God is speaking to me." It is as if God has gently nodded his head in my direction. The knowing, however, is by faith.

Isn't all of this somewhat subjective? I don't believe so. But there is certainly a learning curve involved. Initially, we take a step in faith by listening, and increasingly, a greater clarity and confidence comes in hearing. Gradually, a sureness develops about when the Spirit is speaking. Many seasoned Christians indicate that over time they have learned to listen, and they now know when God is speaking.

This concept alarms some Christians who fear that such promptings will lead us into dangerous waters. But in our listening, we always have the written Word as a safeguard. The promptings of the Holy Spirit that we've been discussing must align with what God has already said in the Bible. The Bible must be the standard by which we weigh what we hear.

Listen to God's command to the disciples in Matthew 17:5: "This is my Son, whom I love; with him I am well pleased. Listen to him!" I believe God still wants to speak to us as individuals and couples. Yes, he speaks through his written Word, but he will also speak through his Spirit to us. We will have to listen carefully, but the question really becomes, will we pause long enough to hear at all?

A Hearing Heart

Judson Cornwall traces the importance of listening to God back to the Bible:

> Daniel was in prayer each time a divine revelation was given to him. Paul speaks of being in prayer when revelation was given, and John was in prayer on the Isle of Patmos when the great revelation of Jesus Christ was given to him. God reveals His will, His word, His work and His ways through the prayer channel.[10]

God speaks to his people through prayer. Peter's example in Acts 10 is but one illustration. He went up to his rooftop for his usual time of prayer. On this particular day, however, God gave Peter an important revelation. Because Peter obediently prayed, God had the opportunity to speak to him. God is *still* speaking!

How can couples practically listen to God while praying together? First, we must recognize and incorporate this aspect of prayer into our prayer time. Listening needs to become a regular part of our time with God. This might seem artificial and cumbersome. After all, can't God speak to us at any point in our time of prayer? Certainly. God has a habit of interrupting us sometimes to direct our prayers or to reveal himself in some way. Then, too, we ourselves may choose to pause for a moment at any time in our prayer to hear from God or to sense his presence. But if we are learning how to listen to God, creating a specific time when we practice listening may help us. Even couples who are seasoned in prayer often like to create a specific time for waiting on the Lord, for experiencing his presence and being open to his Spirit.

Naomi and I first learned about listening together for God's

voice when we thrashed out some of the first decisions of our marriage. During our first two years of marriage, I was a school teacher.
Just before that third year, we had to decide whether to leave my
secure teaching job and help begin a full-time faith ministry —
meaning there wouldn't be a regular paycheck! We had to decide
whether or not to go ahead. Naturally we were praying a great deal
about this decision.

Often we'd pray for wisdom. But we'd also ask God, "Father,
show us what direction you want us to go. Should we join this new
ministry?" Then we would wait for an answer. We would spend perhaps a few minutes being silent, trying to rid our minds of our own
ideas and be sensitive to God. This happened often.

Did God answer? Yes. The "divine whisper" came. God seemed
to be saying, "This is my path for you." I quit my teaching job and
we spent three years in a ministry that had much less financial security. God demonstrated his faithfulness to us throughout those years.
He confirmed over and over that he had whispered his way to us,
that we had heard him correctly. That experience was only the beginning of our journey in trying to listen to God for his direction, his
encouragement, and his challenge.

Joyce Hugget describes a couple's passage toward listening prayer
in her book *The Joy of Listening to God:*

> Tom once described how this process of listening to God
> had turned his marriage inside out. While listening to God
> on one occasion, he sensed that God was urging him to ask
> his wife's forgiveness for the way he had failed in the past.
> That night, he made his confession and suggested that he and
> his wife should be quiet together. The result of this act of
> obedience was that his wife rededicated her life to Christ.

From that time on, Tom and his wife set the alarm for 6 A.M. every morning so that they could enjoy a time of quiet together. They would read the Bible, pray and listen for God's still, small voice. Whenever they sensed God was speaking to them, they would write down the instructions or challenges or directions they received. They determined to obey to the best of their ability. Their love for one another deepened, their marriage was enriched, and the new quality of their lives touched their many friends and acquaintances.[11]

Many couples find it helpful to think of listening prayer in terms of three stages.

Quietness

François Fenélon begins our discussion:

> Be silent, and listen to God. Let your heart be in such a state of preparation that his Spirit may impress upon you such virtues as will please him. Let all within you listen to him. This silence of all outward and earthly affection and of human thoughts within us is essential if we are to hear his voice.[12]

Until a few years ago, we lived on a hill above a little town that had a train track running through it. Trains would run on that track all day, but most of us simply didn't notice the sound that accompanied their presence. It wasn't until our work was done for the day and we sat down to relax at night that we noticed the trains. In our hurrying and busyness, we didn't hear what was there to be heard all along. As soon as we were quiet, we could hear the trains moving through the valley. In our silence, we listened.

This is the best reason for a stage of quietness in our prayers.

Many times we are too busy to hear God. The radio, the television, and the sound of our own minds can literally drown out God's voice. We need to "be still, and know that I am God" (Psalms 46:10). If we are silent, we can listen! The importance of being quiet is emphasized by Joyce Huggett:

> Until our bodies, minds and spirits let go of the clutter we bring to our places of prayer, we automatically tune out the still, small voice of God. Unless we come into stillness before God we do not detect either the fullness of his presence or the winsomeness of his voice.[13]

One way we as couples can prepare to listen for God's voice is to let go of the clutter in our lives by quieting ourselves. This means to relax our bodies and minds and to calm our hearts. The Quakers call this "centering down," which means to release any distractions from our minds and to center our full attention on God. One husband told me that he always keeps a pad and pen close by during times of prayer and listening so that he can jot down the things that might be buzzing in his mind that he needed to do later. This reduces his distractions and allows him to focus on God.

As we actively listen for God's voice, we can pray, "Father, help us now to be still and to let go of the distractions." When we've been able to be quiet before the Lord for a moment and have been able to let go of our tensions and anxieties, it's time to move on to stage two.

Awareness

The object of this stage is to become acutely aware of God's presence. One way to do that is to recall and meditate upon the Scriptures that describe who God is. Jeremiah 31:3, Romans 8:38–39, and Psalms 91 are only a few portions of Scripture that can help us enter God's presence. Personalize these Scriptures. For example, Psalms 91 might be prayed: "Because we dwell in the shelter of the most High, we are resting in the shadow of the Almighty." As you meditate, see yourself close to God, resting in his presence. Begin to recognize the reality of God's presence with you!

Another way to become aware of God is to begin to thank him that he is with you at that very moment, that he indwells you by his Spirit; that you never walk alone. As you thank him, open yourselves as a couple to his presence in your lives. Surrender yourselves to him anew. Bask in the light of his love for you. In one way or another, help make real to yourselves the fact that God is actually there with you, that his arms are around you.

Combining stages one and two, Richard Foster suggests:

> Begin by seating yourself comfortably and then slowly and deliberately let all tension and anxiety drop away. Become aware of God's presence in the room. Perhaps you will want to picture Jesus sitting in the chair across from you, for he is indeed truly present.[14]

Receptiveness

At some point, you will be ready to listen to God and receive from him. This won't necessarily happen right away. We can't hear God when our minds are full of other things. God will speak as we quiet our hearts and spend time in his presence. In my experience, this doesn't happen every time I am quiet before him. Sometimes Naomi and I may spend time listening and come away with a sense simply that he is there. At other times, one or both of us might hear something from the Lord.

His Message

What does God say? What can we expect to hear from him? First let me suggest what we must *not* expect. We know that God will not say anything that contradicts or supersedes his written Word, the Bible. A new doctrine or a modification of a command will not be part of any message from God. Revelation 22:18 is but one verse that affirms the Bible is a finished work. If we're hearing something contrary to God's Word, we should check our spiritual ears!

This point is worth reemphasizing: What we hear must align itself with what God has already spoken through his written Word, the Bible. This caution protects us from both the deception of the evil one and our own selfish hearts.

When my wife and I listen together, we have each other to confirm what God is saying. This too brings safety. But I would rather err and have to be brought back to center (which of course, God gently does in his own way), than shut my ears to God's voice.

Naomi and I find that when God speaks, we generally hear either encouragement, direction, or correction. Sometimes when we are tired or discouraged, God gently affirms his love for us. When we come with a need for an answer in prayer, we ask God to show us the specific direction he wants us to take. At still other times, God may challenge us with something he wants us to be or do.

Encouragement, direction, and correction are three kinds of communication from God that we see all through the Bible. I think of the encouragement God gave to Joshua: "Be strong and courageous. Do not be terrified; do not be discouraged, for the LORD your God will be with you wherever you go" (Joshua 1:9). To Jeremiah, "Do not say, 'I am only a child.'... Do not be afraid of them, for I am with you and will rescue you" (Jeremiah 1:7–8). Throughout the

Bible, God speaks encouragement to his people. Naomi and I have heard many encouraging words from God over the years.

In Acts 9, God gave Ananias specific directions about Paul. Since God has a will for our lives, it is reasonable to assume he will continue to give us direction when we ask for it. Naomi and I have asked God for concrete direction and then listened for his answer. As a result, we have been challenged by God over and over to walk a certain way.

Correction is also a part of what God speaks to his people; God helps us see that we have sinned or gone astray. Jesus talked about the Spirit's work by saying that he would "convict the world of guilt in regard to sin and righteousness and judgment" (John 16:8). We all know what it means for the Spirit to speak to us about sin in our lives. This may happen while we're praying together with our spouse.

Sometimes, God seems to combine these elements. One message that God gives many characters in the Old and New Testament is a combination of encouragement and direction. He told Paul, "Do not be afraid; keep on speaking, do not be silent. For I am with you, and no one is going to attack or harm you" (Acts 18:9–10).

Of course, God might also wish to speak to couples about the needs of others, particularly in knowing how to pray for them. As we listen, we must be open and sensitive to God's voice. In whatever way God speaks, we want to be open to his voice and to the loving relationship he yearns to have with us.

When God Speaks

A booming voice from heaven would make hearing God a lot easier. As it is, we must sort through the voices that echo in our mind and discover if any of them belong to him. It's tricky. People will tell you everything from "listen to your own good sense" to "I just got a divine revelation." In spite of the confusion, God promises we can know his voice. Let's talk about listening to him.

Where We're At (both answer)

1. When it comes right down to it, are you sure God talks to you? If yes, what helps you determine his voice. If no, why not?

Prompter: Consistency with Bible, need for a booming voice...

2. Do you have a quiet, listening time in your prayers? If not, why?

Prompter: Comfort level, mind on track, not tried it...

3. Even though you feel you hear God most of the time, are there situations or issues that make it harder for you to "hear" him?

4. If you're unsure about your ability to hear God, what might make you feel more confident of his voice?

A Step Forward

Based on the "hearing" strengths and weaknesses you've told each other, share one way that being prayer partners can help confirm God's voice.

Prompter: I need help when discerning _____.

"Closet" Action

Pray together about an issue you now face. Make an effort to use the stages of listening that are discussed in this chapter: quietness, awareness of God's presence, and listening/receiving. During your last stage, write down any thoughts that come to mind. When you've finished praying, discuss what you wrote. If your paper's empty, that's fine. This is only an exercise, not a command performance by God.

Keeping Prayer Vital

Be joyful always, pray continually...
1 THESSALONIANS 5:16–17

MANY YEARS AGO, GOD USED A BIBLE TEACHER'S simple instruction to lead Naomi and I to a new commitment to prayer in our lives. That's when we decided to apply ourselves to a daily prayer regimen. Each day we conscientiously prayed through a series of prayer laps together. This discipline brought about a revival in our prayer lives together.

It was wonderful at first, and we learned much from our experience. But after praying together for a year, using the same format, praying for many of the same concerns every day — we experienced a kind of prayer burnout. Our time with God seemed to lack spontaneity. We wondered how we would keep our prayer life meaningful.

Whenever we learn a new skill, or enter a new dimension in our lives, we're full of enthusiasm. But any activity can become boring, repetitive, and even meaningless over time. How can we keep our prayer times together vital, alive, and growing? Here are some ways that have helped a number of couples. This list isn't exhaustive — you may come up with some great ideas of your own — but if your prayers together become routine and predictable, it's time to consider some options. Some of these suggestions may help you light that flame again.

One Thing at a Time

We've found that focusing on just one aspect of prayer at a time helps to break us free from a stale routine. You can concentrate on thanksgiving by considering the attributes of God. Or immerse yourself into praise by reading Psalms, or singing worship songs. You can simply reflect on what God has done for you and your spouse. On a couple of occasions, Naomi and I have gone back through our entire marriage and thanked God for specific ways in which he's worked in our lives: "Thank you, Lord, for working out a scholarship for Naomi." "Thank you for healing Naomi's cancer." "Lord, thanks so much for making a way for Art to go to seminary."

At other times we might concentrate on petition or intercession. Spend a few moments before prayer asking each other about specific needs, going beneath the surface to find how you can effectively pray for each other. Center on those needs during your prayer time. Sometimes we just pray for our kids, our extended family, or our church. Occasionally we just quiet ourselves before God, and listen for his voice or meditate on Scripture. Ask God to help you become more creative in your prayers — after all, he's the mighty Creator, and he's the one you're praying to.

Keep a Prayer Notebook

Sometimes couples spend a lot of time praying for the same situations every day. Family, friends, church, and community all generate needs that require faithful intercession. But since life doesn't always change quickly, we might find ourselves praying about these situations by rote — without much personal involvement or emotion. Nothing will kill our enthusiasm for praying together more quickly.

You might also struggle with keeping track of all the requests. "Could you pray for me this week?" someone asks. We say yes, but may forget to pray. Sometimes there are so many concerns at church, among our friends, and in our community that we simply can't keep track of it all.

A prayer notebook might be the answer for both of these problems. It helps us record prayer requests and provides a method for praying regularly without citing every need every day.

If you want to begin a prayer notebook, obtain a refillable binder. Use one sheet of paper for each request. For example, "John Smith: Needs employment, 1/8/96." On that page you can also write items that will allow you to pray very specifically: "Job interview 2/17/96."

Put four dividers in the notebook, one labeled "Daily," one labeled "Regular," one labeled "Answered," one labeled "Inactive."

In the section labeled "Daily," insert the pages for items that you want to pray for all the time. These are matters requiring immediate attention. In the "Regular" section, insert the pages for items that you want to pray for regularly, but not necessarily all the time. When a prayer request is answered, move its page to the section labeled "Answered." When a request hasn't been answered but you don't know whether you want to continue praying about it, place it in the "Inactive" section. It will be available if you're led to begin praying about it again.

When it's time to intercede in your prayers, use the items in the "Daily "and "Regular" sections to remind you of what you want to pray about. Pray for every item in the "Daily" section and some of those in the "Regular" section. Decide how many you want to pray for in the "Regular" section each day. Say you want to pray for four requests from the "Regular" section; simply flip through the requests during your time of intercession. Place a marker after your last request, so that the next time you pray you can begin where you left off. Occasionally go to the "Answered" section and thank God for his provision.

Too mechanical, you say? Like all techniques, this method is not for everyone. However, many couples find a prayer notebook keeps their prayer time vital because it releases them from the anxiety of missing a prayer need and the boredom of praying for the same things every day.

Hiding the Word in Your Hearts

Meditative prayer can be a wonderful way to understand the Lord's heart. Simply use the Scripture as a guide to your prayer time. Find a meaningful passage or series of related verses and talk with God about them. Perhaps they will lead you to thank God for what he's provided, or to pray the passage into your life, or to ask for insight.

Paul Stevens' wonderful meditation for couples, found in his book *Married for Good* is a great example of how to use Scripture in meditation and prayer:

Show Your Love Again
A Meditation for Couples

Use the following meditation with your spouse as a guided meditative prayer.

1) God made us. "For you created my inmost being; you knit me

together in my mother's womb" (Psalms 139:13). Thank God that He created you and your spouse to be the unique person you are.

2) God made us in His image (Genesis 1:26–27). Thank God that He made you to be a creative expression of Himself.

3) God made us male and female (Genesis 1:27). Thank Him for the difference.

4) God made us from each other and for each other (Genesis 2:22). The woman was taken out of the man and the man found himself again in the woman. Thank God that the woman was not made to be an assistant man but to be a helper as his opposite and he to her.

5) The Lord God brought the woman to the man (Genesis 2:22). How did you find each other? What brought you together? Thank God that He was involved in bringing you to each other.

6) The man and his wife were both naked and were not ashamed (Genesis 2:25). Thank God for the capacity He has given you to say "I love you" with your body, soul and spirit. Thank Him for those times when there has been nothing between you (and your spouse), when communication has been open.

7) The man and his wife knew they were naked and made coverings for themselves (Genesis 3:7). Recognize what sin does to your intimacy and how futile it is to cover yourself with self-justification, a pretense of strength or weakness, roles or masks.

8) The Lord God made garments of skin for Adam and his wife and clothed them (Genesis 3:21). Thank God that you can risk being completely honest with all that is inside you because Christ covers you.

9) God said: Go show your love to your spouse again (Hosea 3:1). If some coldness has set in, if the little kindnesses have long

vanished, if you are beginning to think that someone else may be more understanding, hear this word! God says, "Show your love again." Invite God to help you to find your spouse emotionally again and to show love.

10) Wives submit to your husbands as to the Lord. Husbands love your wives as Christ loved the church. Submit to one another out of reverence for Christ (Ephesians 5:22, 25, 21). Thank God that your relationship is a sacramental means of expressing the relationship of Jesus with His people. Pray that in mutual submission you may increasingly find a way of being husband or wife to God's glory.

11) What God has joined together let man not separate (Matthew 19:6). Will you forever renounce the thought of seeking a way out of the relationship? Rest, even rejoice, that you are committed until death parts you.

12) Though one may be over-powered, two can defend themselves. A cord of three strands is not quickly broken (Ecclesiastes 4:12). Consciously welcome the "third strand" in your marriage — the living Christ. Give Him permission to be interwoven with you. Let His strength and love bind you together.

13) God is love and he who dwells in love dwells in God (1 John 4:16). Thank Him that you can be anywhere with anyone and experience the highest joy of a human being: to dwell in God and to be indwelt by God.[1]

Stevens' meditation is quite extensive but might be a wonderful tool to help you vary your prayer time. If it seems too long to do in one sitting, try using one part of it at a time. Meditative prayer can put us in better touch with God's heart and encourage us to yield our hearts to him.

Share Your Hearts

Relating to God has to do with the privilege of expressing our thoughts, emotions, and ideas to him. These may have nothing to do with intercession, petition, or even praise, but they are a real part of communion with God.

Psalms 62:8 describes this aspect of prayer: "Trust in him at all times, O people; pour out your hearts to him, for God is our refuge." Many of the Psalms are an outpouring of the emotions and thoughts of a believer. They show us how God's children have shared with him what they were feeling and thinking.

This kind of communication is appropriate at any time during prayer. While interceding for our children, we may share our anxiety about a particular child, our feelings of love and concern. Perhaps while praying for forgiveness, we also will talk to God about our pain and sense of frustration. "Pour out your hearts," the psalmist says.

This concept is aptly demonstrated by Anselm of Canterbury, a tenth-century monk who prayed: "I am frightened of living, Lord. My whole seems sinful or sterile though I fear you, I trust you."[2] What a pouring out of emotion to God!

If prayer is becoming stiff and non-relational, perhaps you need to consider sharing your heart with God. Are you willing to pour out your heart? God will listen; you can trust him. And as you share your heart with both God and your spouse, you'll see the level of intimacy in your marriage rise.

Learn More about It

If you find that you are not growing in your prayer life as a couple, why not take advantage of what others have experienced in the area of prayer? Choose a book to read together and discuss it as you go.

Try to incorporate what you are reading into your prayer life, when it is appropriate for you. You will find a number of titles in the notes which follow this chapter that might be a great starting place.

One on One

Each of us has a personal relationship with God as an individual. That relationship is nurtured and grown in the environment of prayer. When husbands and wives don't pray individually, they are much less likely to pray with their spouse.

Spend a few moments going beneath the surface to find how you can effectively pray for each other.

When a couple forms that one new world, God must occupy its center and prayer must be its common language.

Time dictates that only so many extended times of prayer can fit into one week. How do we find the right balance between individual prayer and praying together? Each couple must decide what is comfortable for them. What works will vary over time according to the season of our marriage and how much time we have in our schedule. But if either type of prayer is neglected, our relationship with God and with each other may be affected. Keep prayer vital by finding the balance.

Never Give Up

Mike Mason offers an apt description of marriage: "A marriage is not a joining of two worlds, but an abandoning of two worlds in order that one new one might be formed."[3] When a couple forms that one new world, God must occupy its center and prayer must be its common language.

Form that new world together! Be active in inviting God into your relationship as a couple. Learn the language of praying together. As you do, experience the warmth of God's presence and the excitement of a shared spiritual journey. There is joy in the road ahead. Invite God into your relationship through prayer and find a growing sense of his presence in your lives.

Habit Verses Heart

The habit of praying together can bring intimacy, faith and strength. But without careful nurturing it can also bring ritual without heart — meaningless words and boredom. In this chapter we've discussed guarding our hearts from mere habit. Go over the following questions to make it personal.

Where We're At (both answer)

1. When you pray together, have you ever noticed times when your heart shut off, or your words became the expected thing to say? If yes, when?

Prompter: Tired, tuned out…

2. Often prayer feels less needful (relevant) when things are going well. Why do you think this is? Any ideas on how to get past the feeling?

Prompter: Something different, thanks only…

3. From past experience, do you think "dry" times are a part of the Christian's life? If so, why does God allow them? Do they have value?

A Step Forward

Tell your partner a way that he or she can help you when you struggle with dryness or boredom.

Prompter: On guard for drifting into a stale habit…

"Closet" Action

Thank God for giving you your prayer partner. Tell him why he or she is important to your spiritual life. Then ask his Spirit to help preserve and grow the amazing gift that he's given you. Ask him to make you sensitive to empty words or a cooling heart. Invite him to spark creativity and life into your prayer times together!

Chapter One: What Happens When Couples Pray?

1. Robert Van de Weyer, ed., *The HarperCollins Book of Prayers* (New York: HarperCollins, 1993), 213.

2. Paul Stevens, *Marriage Spirituality* (Downers Grove, Ill.: InterVarsity, 1989), 75.

3. James Houston, *The Transforming Friendship* (Batavia: Lion Publishers, 1989), 303.

4. Grant Osborne, interview by author, Deerfield, Ill., 6 October 1995.

5. Alan M. Stibbs, *The First Epistle General of Peter,* Tyndale New Testament Commentaries, no. 17, ed. R. V. G. Tasker, (Grand Rapids: Eerdmans, 1981), 127.

6. Carol Zetterberg and Larry Zetterberg, "In the Prayer Chair," *Guideposts* (February 1993), 30-33.

Chapter Two: Getting Closer to the One You Love

1. Mike Mason, *The Mystery of Marriage* (Portland, Ore.: Multnomah, 1985), 74.

2. Ken Druck, *The Secrets Men Keep* (New York: Doubleday, 1985), 13.

3. M. Scott Peck, *People of the Lie* (New York: Simon and Shuster, 1983), 60.

4. Gary Smalley and John Trent, *The Blessing* (Nashville: Nelson, 1986), 9-20.

5. *Search for Significance* by Robert McGee is a helpful book in this area.

6. Houston, *Transforming Friendship,* 33-34.

7. Brother Lawrence, *The Practice of the Presence of God,* 60.

8. Van de Weyer, *Book of Prayers,* 361.

9. A. W. Tozer, *The Pursuit of God* (Harrisburg, Penn.: Christian Publications), 12-13.

Chapter Three: Pray As You Can, Not As You Can't

1. O. Hallesby categorizes prayer into the major areas of supplicatory prayer, the prayer of thanksgiving, praise, conversation, and prayer without words.

2. Dick Eastman's list includes the following: praise, waiting, confession, Scripture praying, watching, intercession, petition, thanksgiving, singing, meditation, listening, praise.

3. Judson Cornwall sees prayer as a channel for confession, petition, communication, intercession, the release of faith, submission, thanksgiving, and praise.

4. Richard J. Foster and James Bryan Smith, eds. *Devotional Classics* (New York: HarperCollins, 1993), 133.

5. Richard J. Foster, *Prayer* (New York: HarperCollins, 1992), 200.

6. Stibbs, *First Epistle of Peter,* 74.

7. Bill Hybels, *Too Busy Not to Pray* (Downers Grove, Ill.: InterVarsity, 1988).

8. Van de Weyer, *Book of Prayers,* 234.

Chapter Four: Finding Time without Adding Pressure

1. Foster, *Prayer,* 13.

2. Ibid., 13-14.

3. Stephen R. Covey, *The Seven Habits of Highly Effective People* (New York: Simon and Shuster, 1989), 157-58.

4. Stevens, *Marriage Spirituality,* 25.

Chapter Six: Restoring Broken Relationships

1. Gary Smalley, *The Joy of Committed Love* (Grand Rapids: Zondervan, 1984), 66.

2. Lewis B. Smedes, "Forgiveness: The Power to Change the Past," *Christianity Today* (7 January 1983): 22-26.

Chapter Seven: Gaining Peace in Times of Crisis

1. B. M. Palmer, *Theology of Prayer* (Harrisonburg: Sprinkle, 1980), 15.

2. Ibid., 16.

3. Veronica Zundel, ed., *Eerdman's Book of Famous Prayers* (Grand Rapids: Eerdmans, 1983), 43.

4. O. Hallesby, *Prayer* (Minneapolis: Augsburg, 1931), 17.

5. Lawrence O. Richards, *Expository Dictionary of Bible Words* (Grand Rapids: Zondervan, 1985), 498.

6. Foster, *Prayer,* 183-84.

7. Hallesby, *Prayer,* 52.

Chapter Nine: Resisting the Evil One

1. Thomas B. White, *The Believer's Guide to Spiritual Warfare* (Ann Arbor, Mich.: Vine Books, 1990), 21.

2. Thomas B. White, *Breaking Strongholds* (Ann Arbor, Mich.: Vine Books, 1993), 24.

Chapter Ten: Hearing God's Voice

1. Foster and Smith, *Devotional Classics,* 322-23.

2. Zundel, *Famous Prayers,* 27.

3. Philip Yancey, "From Carnival to Mardi Gras," *Christianity Today* (26 April 1993): 64.

4. Tozer, *Pursuit of God,* 13-14.

5. Foster, *Prayer,* 28.

6. Ibid., 93.

7. Van de Weyer, *Book of Prayers,* 381.

8. White, *Breaking Strongholds,* 66.

9. Tozer, *Pursuit of God,* 78-79.

10. Judson Cornwall, *The Secret of Personal Prayer* (Altamonte Springs, Fla.: Creation House, 1988), 84.

11. Joyce Hugget, *The Joy of Listening to God* (Downers Grove, Ill.: InterVarsity, 1986), 21.

12. Foster, *Prayer,* 163.

13. Hugget, *Listening to God,* 55.

14. Foster, *Prayer,* 161.

Chapter Eleven: Keeping Prayer Vital

1. Paul Stevens, *Married for Good: The Lost Art of Staying Happily Married* (Downers Grove, Ill.: InterVarsity, 1986).

2. Van de Weyer, *Book of Prayers,* 32.

3. Mason, *Mystery of Marriage,* 91.

Reading List

Barclay, William. 1990. *A Barclay Prayer Book*. Trinity Press: International.

Cornwall, Judson. 1988. *The Secret of Personal Prayer*. Altamonte Springs: Creation House.

Eastman, Dick. 1978. *The Hour that Changes the World*. Grand Rapids: Baker.

Foster, Richard J. 1992. *Prayer*. New York: HarperCollins.

Foster, Richard J. and James Bryan Smith, eds. 1992. *Devotional Classics*. New York: HarperCollins.

Hallesby, O. 1931. *Prayer*. Minneapolis: Augsburg.

Houston, James. 1989. *The Transforming Friendship*. Batavia: Lion Publishers.

Hugget, Joyce. 1986. *The Joy of Listening to God*. Downers Grove: InterVarsity.

Mason, Mike. 1985. *The Mystery of Marriage*. Portland: Multnomah.

Murray, Andrew. 1982. *The Believer's School of Prayer*. Minneapolis: Bethany.

Murray, Andrew. 1982. *Ministry of Intercessory Prayer*. Minneapolis: Bethany.

Payne, Leanne. 1994. *Listening Prayer: Learning to Hear God's Voice & Keep a Prayer Journal*. Grand Rapids: Baker.

Roberts, Lee. *Praying God's Will for My Marriage*. Nashville: Thomas Nelson.

Smalley, Gary. 1984. *The Joy of Committed Love*. Grand Rapids: Zondervan.

Smalley, Gary, and John Trent. 1986. *The Blessing*. Nashville: Nelson.

Smalley, Gary, and John Trent. 1988. *The Language of Love*. Pomona: Focus on the Family.

Stevens, Paul. 1989. *Marriage Spirituality*. Downers Grove: InterVarsity.

Stevens, Paul. 1986. *Married for Good: The Lost Art of Staying Happily Married*. Downers Grove: InterVarsity.

White, Thomas B. 1990. *The Believer's Guide to Spiritual Warfare*. Ann Arbor: Vine Books.

Wright, H. Norman. 1988. *Making Peace With Your Partner*. Dallas: Word.

Wright, H. Norman. 1990. *Quiet Times For Couples*. Eugene: Harvest House.